Mount Zion Cemetery

Aldie
Virginia

Wynne C. Saffer

HERITAGE BOOKS
2006

HERITAGE BOOKS
AN IMPRINT OF HERITAGE BOOKS, INC.

Books, CDs, and more—Worldwide

For our listing of thousands of titles see our website
at
www.HeritageBooks.com

Published 2006 by
HERITAGE BOOKS, INC.
Publishing Division
65 East Main Street
Westminster, Maryland 21157-5026

International Standard Book Number: 978-1-888265-26-4

INTRODUCTION

When visitors stop at Mt. Zion Old School Baptist Church on Route 50 two miles east of Aldie, they can read the marker which stands on the north side of the church:

MT. ZION CHURCH

Mt. Zion Old School Baptist Church was founded in 1851. Just west of the church is a graveyard containing many 19th century grave markers. On July 6, 1864 nearby, Mosby's Rangers attacked and routed 150 Union cavalrymen, over 100 Union soldiers were killed, wounded or captured. Mosby had eight men wounded, one mortally. The church is site of the annual Thomas family reunion founded 1934.

The visitor may then wander through the cemetery and read a few of the inscriptions on the grave markers. Maybe they are looking for an ancestor or maybe they just like the peace and tranquility of an old cemetery. The names and dates are carved into the marble and granite, but who were these people? Did they leave spouses or children behind when they were buried here? Where did they live? Were they members of the old church over the wall? This publication may answer some of those questions. The following is a compilation of death notices, obituaries and community news columns from newpapers published in Loudoun County which refer to the people buried here. The name of those buried in the cemetery are shown in **bold type**. The articles are presented in chronological order. The Alexandria Gazette, which was circulated in Loudoun County, was also used for reports prior to 1880. The microfilm of the actual newspapers are available at the Thomas Balch Library in Leesburg. I have tried to transcribe the notices accurately, but anyone with a greater interest may want to view the original. I have included a few other articles from the paper which relate to Mt. Zion Old School Baptist Church or people or events of the vicinity which were of interest to me. I have also included some family charts to assist the readers in seeing the family connections for some of the people buried here.

There are about 240 graves in the cemetery with inscribed markers, and a listing has been included of those. An asterick (*) was used to indicate if a death notice, obituary or news item relating to their death is included in the text. Also included in the cemetery are several fieldstone markers which mark the graves of others unknown. During the Civil War the church was used as a hospital, and soldiers who died there may have been buried in the cemetery with or without stone markers. The Mount Zion Church Preservation Association has recently placed twelve markers for Union soldiers who died during the fight at Mt. Zion Church on July 6, 1864. It is believed that their bodies were buried here and may still remain.

This work is not intended as a history of the Church. However, some background may be helpful. The Mt. Zion Old School Baptist Church was built in 1851 on land purchased by the trustees in 1850 from the Riticor family. The founding members of the church were members of the Little River Baptist Church which was established in 1768. The members of the Baptist church divided in the 1830's over doctrine. The more conservative members were referred to as primitive, hard-shell, or old school. They did not believe in trying to attract new members with missionaries and Sunday schools. Their members were drawn to the church by their "free will." In the following obituaries, some people are referred to as "members," meaning those who were baptised, thereby joining the church. In contrast, some individuals were "regular attendants," who may never have been baptised and joined the church. My father told me that my grandfather was a "leaner." What is a leaner? Leaners were people who "leaned" to the primitive Baptist beliefs, but who never had the "will" to join the church. As indicated in the obituaries some people buried here were members of Little River Baptist Church or Aldie Methodist Church. There is no indication that membership in the Old School Baptist Church was ever a condition for burial here. I also need to mention the graves outside the cemetery along the south wall. These are believed to be the burial sites of blacks. Only two of the graves have inscribed markers, and they are included in the cemetery listing. From an archaeological review done for the Mt. Zion Church Preservation Association, approximately 34 grave sites were identified. A review of the minutes of the Frying Pan Church at Herndon, which was a companion church with Mt. Zion, shows that the church had both black and white members prior to the Civil War.

Thus said, I leave to you the reader to learn more about those buried here. I hope that this publication will create an interest in learning more about the history of Mt. Zion Old School Baptist Church. For any who would wish to help preserve this site, I encourage you to join the Mt. Zion Church Preservation Association.

ALEXANDRIA GAZETTE
Alexandria, Virginia
Wednesday, June 24, 1863

Mr. L. W. Buckingham, correspondent of the New York Herald, was on Monday killed under the following circumstances. He was coming from Aldie with news of the cavalry fight, and when five miles below that point was chased by guerrillas. He put spurs to his horse, which stumbled and threw him off, breaking his neck and killing him instantly.

ALEXANDRIA GAZETTE
Alexandria, Virginia
Monday, July 11, 1864

Another Exploit of Moseby

WASHINGTON, July 9.--A letter from Annandale, dated July 8, says: "A scout, one hundred and fifty men, from the 2d Massachusetts and 13th New York Cavalry, under command of Major Forbes, went up in the vicinity of Aldie, where they met Moseby with a large force, with a piece of artillery and riflemen. Moseby charged on them killed ten or fifteen and captured nearly the whole party, horses and accoutrements. These horses were well drilled, and of great value to the Government. The cavalry had Spencer's repeating rifles, which will also be of material service to Moseby. On receipt of the news Colonel Lowell started off at midnight with 200 men from the 2d and 13th regiments, and Capt. McPherson of the 16th New York Cavalry joined him at Fairfax and they proceeded to Aldie, where they found twenty-five wounded men and eleven dead. They scoured the country about that region and found it was of no use to pursue Moseby, as he had twelve hours the start of them towards Upperville, where he had taken his prisoners and booty. This has been Moseby's bravest and largest capture, and there is something about it almost unaccountable when we know how efficient this cavalry force has been heretofore the numerous times they have sought Mosby the past year, and the number of captures they have made.

Captain Stone, of the 2d Massachusetts, of Newburyport, is lying dangerously wounded at Centreville.

Thirty Confederates were at Fairfax Court House yesterday, and some nearer our camp. In fact, we are surrounded by guerillas."

ALEXANDRIA GAZETTE
Alexandria, Virginia
Saturday, October 6, 1866

DIED

In Leesburg, on Friday evening last, of Typhoid Fever, Mr. **JOHN KELLY**, aged 28 years. Mr. K, was a member of the Loudoun Guards, and served faithfully as a private soldier in that command throughout the late war.

ALEXANDRIA GAZETTE
Alexandria, Virginia
Thursday, October 14, 1869

DIED

At Tranquility, Loudoun county, Va., on Wednesday, Oct. 7th, Mrs. **SALLIE BRONAUGH**, in the 86th year of her age.

ALEXANDRIA GAZETTE
Alexandria, Virginia
Wednesday, December 6, 1871

DIED

Near Oatland Mills, Loudoun county, Va., November 17th, Mr. **JOHN B. LEE**, aged 38 years.

2

ALEXANDRIA GAZETTE
Alexandria, Virginia
Thursday, August 29, 1872

DIED

At his residence, near Aldie, on Saturday, August 3, 1872, of dropsy, Mr. **JOHN T. LYNN**, a most worthy and valuable citizen of Loudoun county, in the 48th year of his age.

THE MIRROR
Leesburg, Virginia
October 23, 1872

TOURNAMENT--An interesting affair of this kind came off on Saturday last, on the place of Mr. Saffer near Mt. Zion church. Early in the morning a goodly number of knights assembled at the church, with steeds gaily caparisoned, and headed by the Leesburg Brass Band proceeded to the grounds. The field in which the tourney was held is memorable as the scene of a conflict between Col. Mosby's battalion and the forces under command of Maj. Forbes, of the Federal army. Mr. P. P. Powell, of Leesburg, delivered a beautiful and inspiring address to those about to enter the lists, after which the riding commenced, in which the honors were sharply contested for, by those participating. After the contest the company repaired to an adjoining grove where a bountiful repast was spread, and the inner man having been refreshed, the coronation ceremonies were announced; they were gracefully discharged by Mr. Powell. The royal group were represented by Miss Mollie Hogeland, Queen, and Misses Rust, Maddox and Elgin, and Messrs. G. O. and J. W. Ferguson, L. R. Polen, and John Hogeland, the successful knights. The management, under charge of Marshal Dr. T. L. Laws and his assistants, Messrs. R. B. Poulton, W. T. Rogers and C. E. Skinner, was admirable, and to them the company were indebted for a most pleasurable occasion.

ALEXANDRIA GAZETTE
Alexandria, Virginia
Thursday, March 13, 1873

OBITUARY

At his father's residence, in Loudoun county, Va., on the 14th of February, 1873, Mr. **CHAS. A. RITICOR**, in the 32d year of his age.

THE MIRROR
Leesburg, Virginia
Thursday, November 25, 1875

DIED

At her residence, near Mt. Zion Church, in this county, on Monday, the 8th of November, 1875, Mrs. **ELIZABETH HUTCHISON**, widow of the late Sampson Hutchison, in the 88th year of her age.

ALEXANDRIA GAZETTE
Alexandria, Virginia
Monday, February 14, 1876

VIRGINIA NEWS

At a meeting of the citizens of the Oatland neighborhood in Loudoun county, held last week, a resolution was adopted declaring bill No. 61, fixing the tolls on the Leesburg and Aldie Turnpike, now pending before the Virginia House of Delegates, unequal and unjust in its requirements, and protesting against its passage, as its effect would be to cut them off from all intercourse with Leesburg.

DIED

At the residence of Thomas E. Hunton, near New Baltimore, Fauquier county, Va., on Friday, Jan. 28th, Mr. **JAS. C. GREEN**, of "Locust Bottom," Prince William county. The deceased was in his 64th year, and died respected and loved by all his large circle of friends and acquaintances.

4

THE MIRROR
Leesburg, Virginia
Thursday, July 26, 1877

DIED

Near Aldie, Loudoun county, VA., June 29, **CHARLES RITICOR**, after a short illness, in a few days of being 79 years old.

THE MIRROR
Leesburg, Virginia
February 16, 1882

DIED

HIBBS--At the residence of her daughter, January 29th, 1882, Mrs. **Mary Jane Hibbs**, in the 62nd year of her age. She was a faithful mother and a good neighbor, none knew her but to praise her, she was a consistent member of the Methodist Church for thirty years, and died as she had lived trusting in her Lord, and willing and ready to go where sin and sorrow are felt and feared no more.

The subject of this notice was a sufferer for more than seventeen years from the disease which at last proved fatal, yet she offered no word of complaint, and bore her affliction with patience and resignation, gentle unassuming in her manners, and a kind friend, she won the esteem and confidence of all who knew her. The summons to depart found her ready, and to her to live was Christ, but to die was gain.

THE WASHINGTONIAN
Leesburg, Virginia
July 15, 1882

DIED

At her residence, near Aldie, on the 27th of June, Miss **MELINDA RITICOR**, in the 74th year of her age.

THE WASHINGTONIAN
Leesburg, Virginia
August 19, 1882

DIED

At her residence, near Aldie, Loudoun county, Va., Mrs. **MARGARET TRIPLETT**, in the 74th year of her age.

THE MIRROR
Leesburg, Virginia
Thursday, November 5, 1885

DIED

RITICOR--Near Aldie, Oct. 23th, 1885, Mrs. **Susannah Riticor**, wife of Charles Riticor, dec'd, in the 71st year of her age. For nearly ten years she has been a great sufferer from shortness of breath, at times she could not lie down in bed an hour of the night. But her last weeks of life she had a dreadful cough, very much as consumption. Truly we can say a mother has gone that never will be forgotten while memory lasts of the love she cherished for her dear children and grand children. She seemed to cling to earth for nothing else and left a comforting assurance to all, that this world is not our home, where moth and rust doth corrupt. None knew her but to love her, none named her but to praise. She was kind, charitable neighbor and friend to every one, always studying the good of others, of which appreciations were shown in frequent visits by her relatives and friends during her last sickness.

"Dearest mother thou hast left us
We thy loss most deeply feel,
But 'tis God that has bereft us
He can all our sorrows heal."

She is not dead but Sleepeth.

By a Child

6

THE MIRROR
Leesburg, Virginia
Thursday, March 4, 1886

DIED

SAFFER - At the residence of her parents near Aldie, February 25th, 1886, **Viola D.**, youngest daughter of W. T. and Emma R. **Saffer**, aged one year, ten months and twenty-five days.

God in his omnipotence has again thrust in the sickle of death and reaped from our midst the object of our brightest hopes and joys, no more shall her prattling voice be heard in our midst, she is now safely clasped in the arms of her dear Jesus out of the reach of suffering, sorrow, pain and death. We would not, if we could have her come back to this vile world where sin and sorrow reigneth supreme. Dearest parents do not look on this tenement of clay as your loved one, for ere it was laid in the gaping tomb her angel spirit was on yon bright shore in the arms of him that said "suffer little children to come unto me for of such is the kingdom of heaven." We tender our heartfelt sympathy to the bereaved parents and family in their sad affliction, and humbly resign ourselves to the will of him that doeth all things well.

Dearest Viola thou hast left us
Here thy loss we deeply feel,
But 'tis God that has bereft us,
He can all our sorrows heal

Yet again we hope to meet thee
When the day of life had fled,
Then in heaven with joy to greet thee,
Where no farewell tear is shed.

Her angel spirit to heaven fled
And released her from her suffering bed,
She is one of the angel band,
A crown is upon her head a harp is in her hand.

R. S. P.

7

THE MIRROR
Leesburg, Virginia
Thursday, December 30, 1886

DIED

THOMPSON--At his residence near Aldie, on December 17th, 1886, Mr. **EDWARD THOMPSON**, aged 83 years, 10 months and 11 days.

THE WASHINGTONIAN
Leesburg, Virginia
Saturday, October 22, 1887

MURDER TRIAL

In the Circuit Court on Wednesday last, the case of Ida Manly (colored) charged with killing her brother, a boy of 7 years old, in August last, near Mt. Zion Church, was tried. The jury after an absence of about an hour brought in a verdict of murder in the second degree as charged in the indictment, and fixed the term of her imprisonment in the penitentiary at 18 years. J. B. McCabe for the Commonwealth and Jno. M. Orr for the prisoner.

Mr. Orr moved for a new trial, which Judge Keith overruled, and immediately sentenced the prisoner for the time stated in the verdict of the jury.

THE WASHINGTONIAN
Leesburg, Virginia
Saturday, December 17, 1887

DEATH OF AN OLD SOLDIER

Wm. F. Hibbs, died in this county, on Saturday morning last, at 2 o'clock, aged about 70. Mr. H. was a gallant and meritorious soldier in Mosby's Command during the war, and was familiarly known throughout the Battalion as "Major" Hibbs. He was buried on Monday, at Mt. Zion, by some of his former comrades, and all will remember him with affection, as one who never shirked duty, and was always at his post.

THE WASHINGTONIAN
Leesburg, Virginia
Saturday, December 24, 1887

DIED

On Wednesday morning, Dec. 7th, 1887, near Aldie, **Johnny G. Carruthers**, infant son of Joel & Sallie F. Carruthers, age seven weeks and two days.

Little Johnny is safe at rest
On the loving Saviour's breast,
Nothing can ever harm him there,
He's safe within the Shepherds care.

God took him from this world away
To the bright realms of endless day,
Before he ever learned to sin,
The blessed Master said come in.

Little snow white hands are folded
On our little darlings breast,
Little bright eyes closed forever,
Darling Johnny is at rest.

AUNTIE

THE MIRROR
Leesburg, Virginia
Thursday, March 22, 1888

ALDIE LETTER

Aldie, March 19th, 1888

Mr. Editor: Nothing unusual has happened during the past week to disturb the harmony of our quiet little town, but a protracted visit from old "Boreas," who made things lively by his appearance. Miss Lina Jones, who has been a victim of the terrible disease of Consumption for over a year, died Sunday, the 11th; her remains were interred in Alexandria. Mr. R. L. Sanford had two horses seriously, and perhaps fatally injured, by the running away of his six-horse team near here on Friday last. The fisherman of the town have been completely distanced by Mr. Samuel Fry, of Oatlands, who on Monday last netted a huge monster, weighing 15 pounds and measuring two and a half feet. We are glad to learn that our Graded School will run three months yet. Mr. **John Riticor**, an old and estimable citizen living a few miles from this place, died on Sunday last at an advanced age.   Mr. John Hutchison, whose illness was reported in my last correspondence, is convalescent. The youngest child of J. F. Simpson is in a very serious condition. It was whispered around a few weeks ago, that a Debating Society was to be organized shortly. What has become of it? Mr. Joel Carruthers living a few miles south of here, is very sick with pneumonia.

"JULIET"

THE WASHINGTONIAN
Leesburg, Virginia
Saturday, February 20, 1892

DEATH OF CONFEDERATE VETERAN

Mr. **L. F. Palmer**, a well known merchant at Gum Spring, in this county, died from the effects of the grip followed by pneumonia. He was in the 62d year of his age. In 1861 he enlisted with the Sixth Virginia Cavalry, where he served his State gallantly until the end of the service. He leaves a wife and five children. His funeral took place from Mt. Zion Baptist church.

THE MIRROR
Leesburg, Virginia
Thursday, January 25, 1894

SAFFER - Died at his home, near Aldie, Va., January 17, 1894, Mr. **W. T. Saffer** in his 69th year. When the announcement of his death was passed from man to man in this community, it was apparent even to the heedless child, that sorrow, recognizing few bounds, would invade other homes than the one in which death's victim lay, to proud a place did the deceased hold in the hearts of those who knew him best. Our friend, in life, like all men of character, had his friendships and animosities--decided in both--but manly, fearless, true and self-sacrificing, respecting the former, reticent, just, regarding the latter. In everything that pertained to life's offices, he measured up to the standard of a noble manhood, embodying as he did, all the virtues of an esteemed friend, kind neighbor, indulgent father, and considerate husband. We will miss his stalwart form, pleasant manner, and genial companionship, and unite with the bereaved of the home-circle, in our unfeigned sorrow.

F.

THE WASHINGTONIAN
Leesburg, Virginia
Saturday, January 25, 1896

DEATH OF A GOOD MAN

The death of our old and highly esteemed friend, Mr. **Matthew P. Lee**, was not unexpected, as he was well known as one of our oldest citizens, whose health had been failing for some time. He lived to the good old age of over ninety-one years, and during his long life no one fulfilled the duties of an honorable and useful life more fully than he did. He was the model of a good citizen, a most conscientious business man, and a popular and kind neighbor and friend. The rest of his family have gone to the other world before him, only two children surviving him: Mr. A. H. Lee and Miss Martha Lee. An unusually large number of his friends paid their last sad tribute to his memory by attending his funeral on Sunday, the 26th at Mt. Zion Church, where his remains were buried. Elder J. N. Badger, of the Primitive Baptist Church, officiating.

We have had the most pleasant and satisfactory business relations with Mr. Lee for many years, as he has been a subscriber to this paper for over forty-four years, the time it has been under our management.

THE WASHINGTONIAN
Leesburg, Virginia
Saturday, July 4, 1896

Mrs. **Florence McDonough**, wife of Mr. Thomas McDonough, died at her home in Leesburg on Wednesday evening, July 1st, in the 23d year of her age. She was a daughter of Mr. Morris McFarland of Loudoun county. The young husband has the sympathy of the community in his bereavement. Her funeral took place Friday at Mt. Zion.

THE MIRROR
Leesburg, Virginia
Thursday, August 12, 1897

DIED

SAFFER--Near Aldie, Loudoun County, Va., Mrs. **R. E. Saffer**, wife of Wm. T. Saffer, dec'd, aged 59 years.

Death with its merciless cycle, has again made home desolate; only a little over three years ago, the father, a man of true and noble worth, was taken, and now so soon follows the mother.

'Tis a sore trial to have her go from us. She, who has ever been known for her gentleness, thoughtfulness and christian fortitude. For a year she had been a great sufferer, and though she knew she was a victim to a malady that baffled the most skilled physicians, never did she murmur, but looked beyond this vale of tears, with a longing to be with her Heavenly Father. Her prayer was rest, sweet rest. Though we shall miss her always, yet, we would not recall her.

From the sorrow and pain of this world,
Her soul has been borne,
To the clime where sorrow and pain is unknown,
Amid the bright scenes of that celestial strand,
Her soul will remain while eternity stands.

L. B. S.

THE WASHINGTONIAN
Leesburg, Virginia
Saturday, April 16, 1898

DEATH OF MRS. E. H. VANSICKLER

We regret to learn, through our Aldie correspondent, of the death on Friday last of Mrs. **Margaret Vansickler**, beloved wife of Mr. E. H. Vansickler, at her home in Aldie. Mrs. Vansickler had been ill for about three months and had suffered intensely. She was a lady of lovely christian character and her untimely death will be a source of great sorrow to her relatives and friends, and devoted husband a great blow. He has our sympathy in his bereavement.

Her funeral took place on Sunday at 2 p.m., Elder J. N. Badger officiating. Interment at Mt. Zion church.

THE WASHINGTONIAN
Leesburg, Virginia
Saturday, February 11, 1899

Died at his home near Mt. Gilead, in this county, on Monday, the 6th inst. Mr. **James Clay Jenkins**, son of the late William Jenkins and brother of Mr. W. S. Jenkins, of this town. In the death of Mr. Jenkins the county has lost a good citizen, the community in which he lived a kind neighbor and friend, and his family a devoted husband and father. He leaves a widow and one child, a boy of ten years of age. He was a consistent member of the Old School, or Primitive Baptist Church. His remains were buried at Mt. Zion on Wednesday last.

THE MIRROR
Leesburg, Virginia
October 26, 1899

DEATH OF MR. E. GRIFFITH THOMAS

Aldie, Va., Oct. 18th, 1899. Mr. **Griffith E. Thomas**, one of Loudoun's oldest and most highly respected citizens, died at Bull Run, the home of Mr. Joel Carruthers, near Aldie, on Wednesday, October 11th, in the 87th year of his age. Mr. Thomas had been a man possessed of more than an ordinary constitution, having led a very active life until within a few months of his death. During the past few years he had been subject to an attack of both grippe and pneumonia, leaving his condition somewhat impaired. He had been confined to his room for the past three months and those who nursed and cared for him realized that the end was near, a number of his family being present during the last moments. The deceased, while not a member of any Church, was a man of the highest type, portraying in his life toward his fellow men those attributes of character which make up the pure and true in manhood. He leaves a wife together with three sons and four daughters to mourn the loss of one who had proven a true and devoted husband and father. The remains were interred in the family lot at 'Mt. Zion,' with six of his grandsons acting as pallbearers.

E.

THE RECORD
Leesburg, Virginia
Friday, July 31, 1903

MISS ETHEL FERGUSON DEAD
(Special from Pleasant Valley)

Miss **Ethel Ferguson**, daughter of Mr. Wilson Ferguson, died at the home of her parents on Saturday last, aged 20 years. She had by diligent study prepared herself as teacher in the public schools, and having taught two sessions was seized with that death dealing malady, consumption, returned to her parents only to remain a short period before passing through that "Valley," which David so vividly pictures. A large concourse of friends and relatives met at the residence of her parents on Monday, at 9 a.m. where a few consoling words were spoken by her pastor, Rev. G. W. Popkins, of whose church she had recently become a member. Interment took place at Mt. Zion church on the same day.

THE WASHINGTONIAN AND MIRROR
Leesburg, Virginia
Thursday, September 28, 1905

Mrs. **V. F. T. Green** died recently at her home at Lenah, in the 73rd year of her age. She is survived by two sisters and two brothers, besides a large and prominent family connection. Her remains were interred at Mt. Zion church.

THE WASHINGTONIAN AND MIRROR
Leesburg, Virginia
Thursday, December 14, 1905

THOMAS MUNDAY

Mr. **Thomas S. Munday**, a well known citizen of Broad Run District, died, after an illness of several weeks, at his home, near Lunette, on Thursday last, aged about 60 years. He was an honest, industrious citizen and was generally regarded as a useful man in his community. He is survived by a wife and several children. His remains were interred at Mt. Zion Church on Saturday.

THE MIRROR
Leesburg, Virginia
Thursday, March 15, 1906

EVERGREEN ECHOES

Mud! mud! mud! The roads are just terrible, but they might be worse. Our miller, Mr. V. R. Mitchell, seems to be doing a thriving business. **Mrs. Wm. Demory**, who has been confined to her bed for sometime, doesn't seem to improve very much, if any.

Miss May Wortman spent Wednesday with her sister, Mrs. V. R. Mitchell. Mrs. W. P. Thomas spent Wednesday with Mrs. Wm. Demory. Misses Ross and Susie Daniel spent Saturday afternoon with Misses Edythe and Mildred Maffett.

Mr. James Sauls, who has been attending school in Herndon, was in Evergreen Tuesday. Miss Edythe Maffett spent Sunday with her aunt, Mrs. J. W. Ankers, of "Pleasant View." Mr. and Mrs. Charles Attwell are entertaining at their home a visitor who has come to stay--a little boy.

Our teacher, Miss Rachel Palmer, spent Saturday and Sunday at her home in Aldie. Mrs. L. J. Wortman spent Sunday with her daughter, Mrs. V. R. Mitchell. Mr. Walter Thrift, of Leesburg, with his friend, Mr. Yoeman, paid a flying visit home Sunday. Miss Lelia Ankers spent Saturday with Mrs. B. F. Hurst. Mr. Carl Wortman spent Sunday with relatives near Waterford. Mr. and Mrs. B. F. Hurst spent Sunday afternoon with friends in Waxpool.

AN OLD MAID

THE LOUDOUN MIRROR
Leesburg, Virginia
November 28, 1913

FRANK VANSICKLER

Mr. **Frank Vansickler** died at the home of his son Mr. Joseph Vansickler of Fairfax County on last Wednesday November 19, 1913, of a complication of diseases, in 75th year of his age. His remains were brought to Mt. Zion, Loudoun County for interment. The funeral service was conducted by Elder C. W. Vaughn. The deceased leaves a wife, one daughter and four sons to mourn his loss. He was an honest upright citizen and loved by all who knew him. The deceased was a native of Loudoun County and lived at Arcola, Va., until a few weeks before his death.

THE LOUDOUN MIRROR
Leesburg, Virginia
October 23, 1914

ARCOLA NEWS

The farmers in this section have been detained with their seeding on account of the recent rains. Mrs. C. M. Turman was in Arcola on Saturday. Miss Estelle Fish and Mrs. C. W. Vaughn were in Leesburg on Tuesday. Mrs. Frank Vansickler of Fairfax has been spending sometime with her daughter Mrs. C. J. C. Maffett near here and attending the Old School Baptist Association at Mt. Zion.

Mrs. William Hutchison of Washington, was the guest of her son and daughter-in-law, Dr. and Mrs. C. P. Hutchison last week. Mrs. Kate B. Orrison spent the weekend with Mrs. L. Fish of Mt. Airy. Mrs. J. C. Rust and son Kemper of Taylorstown were the guests of their cousins, Mrs. L. Fish and daughters and Miss Ratrie recently. Quite an interesting sermon was heard at the home of Elder and Mrs. C. W. Vaughn on last Wednesday evening. Elder Cochern of Floyd County conducted the service.

Mrs. Arthur Mankin is on the sick list. Miss Ona Vaughn was in Ashburn on Sunday. A good many of Arcola neighborhood attend Rally day service at Little River Church on Sunday, quite an interesting program was carried out, and much credit is due the pupils of that school. Wedding bells will soon be ringing in this neighborhood. Miss Anna Ramsay and Miss Estelle Fish were in Aldie on last Monday. Miss Ruth Mankin who has been visiting Miss Pearl Rollins near Ashburn has returned home.

THE LOUDOUN MIRROR
Leesburg, Virginia
May 14, 1915

Arcola News

Mr. A. C. Wyckoff of Alexandria, visited her relatives near Arcola recently. Mr. Harry Pangle is making preparations to erect a dwelling house a few miles south of town. Mr. A. R. Mankin has just purchased an automobile, they are getting very numerous around Arcola. Mrs. Dr. C. P. Hutchison and daughter have just returned from a visit to Washington. Mrs. I. Fish who has been quite sick is improving, but not able to leave her room yet. Mr. C. W. Maffett has lately purchased the farm owned by Mr. Lewis Freeman, for $7,000. The little daughter of Mr. and Mrs. F. M. Byrne is quite sick with grippe. Miss Ruth Mankin has returned from a visit to her sister.

Lorraine, the little daughter of Mr. and Mrs. H. W. Ferguson quietly passed away on last Friday, after a lingering illness. Her remains were carried to Mt. Zion Church on Sunday for burial. The funeral was largely attended. The bereaved family have our deepest sympathy.

THE LOUDOUN MIRROR
Leesburg, Virginia
July 21, 1916

Watson Briefs

This community was grieved to hear of the death of Mr. Henry Fairfax, our distinguished friend and neighbor. He will be greatly missed in this vicinity. Ernest Hutchison, second son of Mr. Dorman Hutchison, died of typhoid fever on Tuesday, of last week, aged 17 years. 'Tis sad for one of tender years to be taken just in the bloom of youth. Both families have the sympathy of our community.

Miss Dorothy Knight of Alexandria has been visiting the Misses Mitchell. Mr. Henry Mitchell is making quite an improvement to his residence by putting a porch across the front. Mr. and Mrs. William Turner of "Sailor's Rest" spent Sunday with Mr. and Mrs. W. Crim, of Evergreen Mills. Mr. Lacey Ferguson and Mr. Harry Riticor spent the weekend in Washington. Mr. Roland Legard, of Wheatland, Va. spent Sunday at the home of Mrs. S. M. Thomas.

17

THE LOUDOUN TIMES
Leesburg, Virginia
Wednesday Afternoon, August 22, 1917

WATSON

This community was shocked when the sad news reached us of the death of **Mrs. J. R. Megeath**, of Alexandria, formerly of Loudoun County. She had been a great sufferer for four weeks of typhoid fever. She was buried at Mt. Zion on Friday, August 17th. J. F. Bovey officiated in the absence of Elder Lefferts. Her entire family have the sympathy of all this neighborhood, where she was raised and dearly loved.

THE MIRROR
Leesburg, Virginia
December 3, 1919

MRS. SALLIE M. THOMAS

Mrs. **Sallie M. Thomas**, widow of the late William Phineas Thomas, died suddenly at her home near Watson on Friday evening, November 28, aged 68. While for some time she had seemed to realize that she had not long to live, her death was a severe shock to her family and friends. Her funeral was preached on Sunday at 12:30 in the Mt. Zion church, where she had been a faithful member for many years, by the Rev. H. H. Lefferts. Her remains were laid to rest in the nearby graveyard, her four sons and two nephews acting as pallbearers. She is survived by seven children, Clarence R. and Margaret S., of Charlottesville; Chas. W., of near Aldie; Mabel E., of Leesburg; Henry P., of Washington, and John G., and Susie R. Thomas, at home; four grandchildren, Vestal, Stuart, Rector and Julia Thomas; three brothers, J. T. and E. V. Riticor, of near Watson, and C. F. Riticor, of near Oatlands, and many other relatives and friends.

THE LOUDOUN TIMES
Leesburg, Virginia
October 21, 1920

BELOVED LOUDOUN LADY PASSES AWAY AT AN ADVANCED AGE
Mrs. Mary Megeath Died At Her Aldie Home On Saturday

Mrs. **Mary Purcell Megeath**, widow of the late Alfred Megeath, died at Aldie, this county, at the home of her son-in-law, Mr. J. M. Leith, on Saturday last, and was buried on Sunday at Mt. Zion. Mrs. Megeath was born near Bloomfield, in Upper Loudoun, ninety-two years ago last July, and spent her long and useful life within this county's borders. She was a woman of high Christian character, a devoted mother, a true friend and an ever considerate neighbor. The large number of people who attended her funeral, and the masses of beautiful flowers, sent by friends, that covered the grave within which her body rests, bore mute testimony of the high esteem in which she was held and of the love she had gathered around her. Mrs. Megeath is survived by seven children.

VICTIM OF COPPERHEAD BITE HAS MADSTONE APPLIED
Miss Henrie Walker of Marshall Brought To Squire Tyler's In Aldie For Application

Miss Henrie Walker, of Marshall Virginia, who was bitten by a copperhead snake, while chestnutting on October 10th, was brought to the madstone, at Squire Tyler's, in Aldie, about twenty-four hours later and the stone applied to the wound on her ankle. The stone upon being applied immediately stuck and adhered for forty-eight hours, the swelling in her entire limb, which was greatly swollen when she arrived, having then all been reduced and but little pain being felt around the wound.

THE LOUDOUN TIMES
Leesburg, Virginia
Thursday, November 11, 1920

MR. LUCIEN CARTER MEETS TRAGIC END
Caught in Mill Wheel At Aldie, He Is Crushed To Death

Mr. Lucien A. Carter, one of Aldie's most highly esteemed citizens, met a tragic death on Tuesday, when he was crushed to death in the machinery of the big grinding mill of that town.

Mr. Carter, who had long been the miller there, had started to make some adjustments to the inside mill wheel after having in accordance with his usual custom chocked the big outside mill wheel in order to stop the machinery. Mr. John Moore was working with him on the other side of the wheel when suddenly the big wheel commenced to turn and the machinery was thrown into operation. The chock had given way, Mr. Moore jumped for safety, but Mr. Carter was caught in the spokes of the wheel he was adjusting and with one agonizing cry he was dashed against the mill wall and the timbers above, his death being instantaneous. An examination of his body showed his skull had been crushed, his right arm broken in two places and his shoulders crushed.

The deceased is survived by his wife, and two sons, Mr. Ira Carter and Mr. William Carter, all of Aldie. His funeral took place yesterday from his late home. A coroners jury summoned to view the remains brought in a verdict of unavoidable accidental death.

MR. WILLIAM SILCOTT DIES IN WASHINGTON
Was One of Middleburg's Most Prominent And Highly Esteemed Citizens

Mr. **William Silcott**, one of Middleburg's most highly esteemed citizens, died of Brights Disease, at the home of his sister, Mrs. Thomas, in Washington on Sunday night last and was buried at Mt. Zion, near Aldie, on Wednesday.

Mr. Silcott, who was fifty-seven years of age, was a man of those sterling qualities that go to make up the highest type of citizen. Kind, generous, charitable, of fine business ability and ever considerate of others he occupied a place in his home community and in the affections of its people that cannot well be filled. He is survived by one brother in Texas and four sisters living in the East.

20

THE LOUDOUN TIMES
Leesburg, Virginia
November 11, 1920

NATIVE OF LOUDOUN DIES IN PRINCE WILLIAM
Mrs. Martha Matthew Passed Away At Her Home Near Stone House

Mrs. **Martha Matthew**, a native of Loudoun, died at her home near Stone House, on Wednesday evening last. Mrs. Matthew was born in Loudoun county, on March 10, 1840. She made her residence in Manassas just after the Civil War, and had been living in Prince William up to the time of her death last Wednesday.

THE LOUDOUN TIMES
Leesburg, Virginia
June 29, 1922

IRA C. CARTER
Dealer In Dry Goods, Groceries, Provisions, Meats, Fruits,
Hardware, Tools, Furniture, House Furnishing Goods Of All Varieties

Complete outfitters of the home and of every member of the family. That describes the stores of Mr. Ira C. Carter of Aldie.

Mr. Carter is proprietor and manager of two large, modern and fully stocked stores, which are operated together. This double business, in which one store is supplemental to the other in the providing of everything for the home, was established in 1913. The buildings are well located and excellently adapted to the uses to which they are put, one of them having a floor area of 1,800 square feet and the other of 2,200 square feet.

The stocks carried are selected with an eye to providing most effieiently and most satisfactorily the highest quality groceries, meats, fruits and other foodstuffs; dry goods, notions, ready-to-wear apparel, shoes, hats, etc., giving facilities for outfitting each member of the family from head to foot; and hardware, furniture, etc.

In the furniture department every desirable article for adding to the comforts of home is to be found. A cash and credit business is done in all branches of the business and the promptest and most courteous service is accorded all customers. Three employees who are polite and attentive assist Mr. Carter in the conduct of the business which has hosts of friends and patrons in Aldie and several of the other communities in this section.

THE LOUDOUN TIMES
Leesburg, Virginia
June 29, 1922

ALDIE GARAGE
Completely Equipped Motorists' Service Station
And Accessories Sales Establishment Is That Of
Mr. William Grehan, Who Guarantees All Work Satisfactory

No transaction is complete with Mr. William Grehan, proprietor of the Aldie Garage, until he is certain that his customer is completely satisfied. That is the business policy on which Mr. Grehan bases every activity in his establishment. The policy was laid down five year ago when he established himself in business with the Aldie Garage, an institution which he planned to make noted for the quality of the service given.

He has made a reputation that fully sustains his ideals and he, consequently, is one of the best known and most prominent men in automotive circles in Northern Virginia.

The garage of Mr. Grehan is a large and commodious and handsomely arranged and appointed structure having about 1,000 square feet of floor space for the meeting of every requirement of his patrons. He has storage space for cars, carries a full and varied line of accessories, oils, gas and sundries, and has a repair department in which expert work is done on all makes of cars. He is an experienced and skilled automobile mechanic himself and has been in the automobile business, learning its every phase, for the last twelve years.

The Aldie garage has been in its present location since it was started fives years ago, and it is well-known to every motorist who traverlses Northern Virginia highways.

Mr. Grehan is a native of Fairfax county and has made his home in Aldie for a number of years, being prominent in all forward movements involving the welfare of the community and the surrounding country. He is an advocate of good roads, better schools and a broader spirit of civic pride. Mr. Grehan is a popular and eminent member of the Masonic order.

THE LOUDOUN TIMES
Leesburg, Virginia
Thursday, August 17, 1922

DEATH OF MR. CHARLES E. SKINNER

Mr. **Charles E. Skinner**, 82 years old, a prominent farmer of Little River, near Aldie, Va., died at his late home on Tuesday. He was a consistent member of the Little River Baptist Church. For many years he taught the Hickory Grove School in Prince William County and his pupils always held him in the highest esteem. On Thursday his pupils held a big reunion at the school, which Mr. Skinner was unable to attend on account of illness. He served with distinction in the Civil War and was one of the best known citizens of the county.

He is survived by his wife, two sons and one daughter. Funeral services conducted by Rev. C. Wirt Trainham, will be held from his late home this afternoon. Interment in Middleburg Cemetery.

LOUDOUN TIMES-MIRROR
Leesburg, Virginia
Thursday Afternoon, December 17, 1925

PROMINENT CITIZEN DIES

Mr. **Eugene W. Presgraves**, a prominent merchant of Lenah, this county, died on Tuesday morning after an illness of about four weeks. He was seventy years of age and had been engaged in the mercantile business most of his life. Mr. Presgraves was very popular in the county and was considered one of Loudoun's most substantial citizens. He was one of the directors of the Farmers & Merchants Banking & Trust Co., Inc., of Leesburg.

He is survived by his widow, Mrs. Ida Bradshaw Presgraves, one daughter, Mrs. Don Isbell of Washington and two brothers, Messrs. Walter and Lewis Presgraves of Pleasant Valley.

Funeral services conducted by Rev. George W. Popkins, were held today. Interment was at Mt. Zion church, near Aldie.

LOUDOUN TIMES-MIRROR
Leesburg, Virginia
Thursday, February 11, 1926

ALDIE

Mr. James Peter Skinner died suddenly at the home of his sister, Mrs. Ludwell Hutchison on Tuesday February 3, in the eighty-fourth year of his age. Mr. Skinner who was a Confederate veteran, was born and raised in Aldie, but had spent a good portion of his life in Fairfax county. The funeral was held on Thursday, the interment being in the old family cemetery at Aldie.

The Christian Endeavor meetings which are held every Sunday afternoon are of much interest to the young people of Aldie. Mr. Marshall Carter is very much indisposed. Mr. and Mrs. Douglas Adams and Douglas Junior, of Washington, spent Sunday with Mr. and Mrs. A. P. Megeath. Mr. and Mrs. Walter George of Norfolk, visited Mrs. George's mother, Mrs. Sallie Carruthers last week. Mrs. Mary Pearson has bought the "Diamond Hill" farm near Little River Church. Mr. Henry Goode of Hyattsville, Md., was an Aldie visitor on Tuesday.

LOUDOUN TIMES-MIRROR
Leesburg, Virginia
Thursday Afternoon, February 25, 1926

ANOTHER VETERAN GONE

Mr. **James W. Sinclair**, member of Company A. Mosby's Command, passed away on February 19 at the home of his daughter, Mrs. Clara Sinclair of Fairfax County, in his 94th year. He was buried at 2:00 o'clock Sunday afternoon by the side of his wife and son in Mount Zion graveyard, it being the locality where Mosby's Command defeated and almost exterminated Major Forbes' California Battallion on July 6, 1864.

This deceased veteran was an active participant in this affair. He was a conspucious character in this section of the state, being known as one of the most fearless and bravest of the brave. Danger was his daily companion, he courted and enjoyed contact with it. His physical strength and power of endurance was marvelous. His record is carried high upon the scroll of honor, that all lovers of the brave and true will never cease to cherish. He has left us to re-enter our noble army that long since crossed the dark chasm and is today parading the streets of the Celestial City amidst the strains of ecstatic music and the hallelujah of the entire host.

The small remaining "Rear Guard" of that once invincible Army will soon join them in a perpetual reunion, leaving the "Sons and Daughters of the Confederacy" to perpetuate the justice and achievements of our course. In this they will never fail, no matter how dark the cloud of adverse fortune may become, a rainbow of a peaceful and happy conscience will span the sky, dispel the gloom and banish every moment of care, every pang of sorrow and every vestige of regret.--An Admiring Comrade in Leesburg.

Mr. Sinclair is survived by a son, W. E. Sinclair of Loudoun County, a daughter, Clara of Fairfax County and two brothers, John Sinclair of Missouri, E. L. Sinclair of Fauquier and one sister, Miss Annie Sinclair of Washington, D.C.

LOUDOUN TIMES-MIRROR
Leesburg, Virginia
Thursday, November 26, 1926

FUNERAL FOR MISS ALICE GULICK

Miss Alice Amelia Gulick died November 16 at her home at Lenah, Va. Funeral services were conducted Friday at Mt. Zion Church and interment at Union Cemetery, Middleburg, Elder H. H. Lefferts officiating. Miss Gulick had suffered from asthma for the past five years, her death resulting from an attack of influenza from which she had been ill about ten days. She was the daughter of the late Sanford and Nancy Gulick and was born near Aldie July 30, 1863, having lived all her life in and near that neighborhood. She is survived by two sisters, Misses Ella and Mollie Gulick with whom she lived, two brothers, Messrs. Robert L. Gulick and Sanford Gulick both of near Lenah. Miss Gulick had many friends who will greatly and sorrowfully miss her in the community.

LOUDOUN TIMES-MIRROR
Leesburg, Virginia
December 9, 1926

DIES IN 70TH YEAR

Mr. **James Robert Megeath** of Aldie, Loudoun County, Virginia, died November 2, 1926 at the Alexandria Hospital after a lingering illness. He was in the seventieth year of his age.

Mr. Megeath was married forty years ago to Miss Margaret Riticor who passed from this life ten years ago. Through ill health and infirmities of age, Mr. Megeath had retired from farm life and his last days were spent with his children.

He is survived by one son, Mr. Humphrey Megeath of Washington and three daughters, Mrs. William Grehan, Aldie; Mrs. T. J. Ross, Bluemont, and Mrs. George Hughes, Vienna, also by the following brothers and sisters: Mr. Herbert Megeath, Cedarville; Mr. Alfred Megeath, Aldie; Mrs. Blanche Furr, Aldie; Mrs. Flora Ferguson, Aldie and Mrs. Lillie Ferguson, Herndon; Mrs. Marvin Leith, Aldie.

Funeral services and burial were at Mt. Zion Church, Aldie, Va., Elder H. H. Lefferts officiating.

LOUDOUN TIMES-MIRROR
Leesburg, Virginia
Thursday Afternoon, January 6, 1927

C. W. BARTON DIES

Charles William Barton died December 22, at his home near Arcola after an illness of several days. He was eighty-eight years of age. Mr. Barton was born near Unison where he made his home until twenty-three years ago when he moved to Arcola.

Barton, a Confederate veteran, belonged to Company A, First Virginia cavalry and served four years, during that time he was in many battles, that included Balls Bluff, Manasass, Gettysburg and the John Brown raid at Harpers Ferry, West Virginia. He served throughout the different battles without injury, but suffered the loss of two valuable horses, one of which was shot dead under him.

Barton was twice married. He is survived by his widow, who before marriage was Miss Ella Furr; two daughters, Miss Nellie Barton and Mrs. Eva Flynn and one son, Mr. Charles Barton. From the first marriage are two sons, William and Welby Barton.

Services were conducted by Elder H. H. Lefferts at Mt. Zion Church. Interment at Mt. Zion Cemetery.

LOUDOUN TIMES-MIRROR
Leesburg, Virginia
Thursday Afternoon, January 6, 1927

FINE BASKETBALL TEAM

Above is the Aldie High School basketball sextet--Loudoun's champion court team. The team won its fifty-first consecutive victory at the Leesburg High School court on Monday night by defeating Round Hill High School 33 to 9.

The players from left to right are (upper row) Misses Lillian Everhart, Frances Everhart, Hazel Sudduth, (lower row) Misses Frankie Leith, Olivia Tyler, Maxine Ambler. Mr. W. E. Tyler, principal of the school is coach.

The record made by this team is believed to be the best ever made by a Virginia High School or may probably surpass records made by any school team in the adjoining states.

The Aldie High School girls basketball team, a picture of which appears in this issue of the Times-Mirror has won the Loudoun county school championship for the past three years and appears to have an excellent opportunity of winning the honors in 1927. The picture does not include three players who have since graduated and left school. These players are Frances Hutchison, Estelle Tyler and Ann Moore. It is quite unusual that a team playing a number of games each season over a period of five years has used only nine regular players.

Mr. W. E. Tyler, Jr., principal of the school has coached the team since the 1923-24 session.

STILL NOT FOUND AT TAN YARD

The still captured last week by sheriff Adrian and his aides and which was reported to have been found at Ish's tan yard, it has later been learned, was found at the house occupied by Harry Simms and Lindsay Young, both colored, who live about two miles from the tan yard.

27

LOUDOUN TIMES-MIRROR
Leesburg, Virginia
Thursday Afternoon, March 10, 1927

MR. DAVID EATON DIES

Mr. **David Henry Clay Eaton** died Tuesday, March 8 at the home of his great-nephew, Mr. F. N. Pangle living near White's Ferry, Montgomery Co., Maryland. He had been in failing health for quite awhile and suffered greatly toward the end. He was born in Loudoun County, Va., and died in the 84th year of his age. His wife was Miss Mary Catherine Riticor, the sister of Mr. Joshua L. Riticor now living in Leesburg, but Mr. Eaton survived his wife several years. There were no children. He leaves no brothers or sisters. Mr. Eaton formerly lived near Aldie and also near Mt. Gilead. Funeral services were held Thursday morning at eleven o'clock at Mt. Zion, Elder Lefferts officiating.

LOUDOUN TIMES-MIRROR
Leesburg, Virginia
Thursday Afternoon, July 28, 1927

THOMAS REUNION

On Tuesday, July 19, 1927 the grounds surrounding old Mt. Zion Church were enlivened by a large gathering when the Thomas family assembled. A bountiful luncheon was served on the grounds in picnic style.

The crowd, just fifty in number, consisted of relatives and friends from Bluefield, West Virginia, Charlottesville, Va., Alexandria, Va., Saint Paul, Va., Aldie, Leesburg and different sections of Loudoun and Prince William counties.

Those present by the name of Thomas were Mr. and Mrs. T. B. Thomas, two daughters and four sons, Mr. and Mrs. Claud Thomas, Mr. Elmer Thomas, Mr. H. H. Thomas and two children, Mr. and Mrs. C. R. Thomas and daughters, Mr. Henry P. Thomas, Mr. and Mrs. C. W. Thomas and daughter, Miss Mabel E. Thomas, Mrs. Lillie Thomas and daughter, Dr. and Mrs. J. G. Thomas and daughter and Mrs. S. F. Ellington (nee Miss Margaret Thomas).

LOUDOUN TIMES-MIRROR
Leesburg, Virginia
Thursday, August 4, 1927

CLEAN UP DAY AT MT. ZION

Thursday, August 11 will be clean-up day at Mt. Zion Church, this county. The purpose is to clean the cemetery and church grounds. All who have an interest in the cemetery are requested to meet on that date (or if rainy, the next day, Friday). Everyone is expected to bring a picnic lunch and therefore enjoy an out-door outing while putting the cemetery and grounds in order.

LOUDOUN TIMES-MIRROR
Leesburg, Virginia
Thursday, August 11, 1927

DIES IN FLORIDA

Mrs. **Sarah Davis Van Sickler** died at the home of her son, Mr. E. Holmes Van Sickler at Lakeland, Florida on Saturday, July 30, in eighty-nineth year of her age. Mrs. Van Sickler was the daughter of the late Joseph Davis and was born at Woodburn, this county. She is an aunt of Mrs. Oden N. Casey of Leesburg. Her son, Mr. Holmes Van Sickler was formerly a merchant in this county. The body was interred at Mt. Zion cemetery, near Aldie, Virginia. Mrs. Van Sickler is survived by three sons and one daughter.

LOUDOUN TIMES-MIRROR
Leesburg, Virginia
Thursday, February 16, 1928

PROMINENT LOUDOUN CITIZEN DIES AT ALDIE
William R. Grehan Dies From The Effects Of Pneumonia
Funeral Services Held At Mt. Zion Wednesday

Mr. **William R. Grehan**, a highly popular and well known citizen of this county, died on Monday night of this week from the effects of pneumonia. Mr. Grehan was forty-six years of age. He came to this county from Alexandria City in 1918 and located at Aldie where he entered into the garage business which he successfully conducted until the time of his death.

Mr. Grehan was married to Miss Effie Megeath in November, 1916. She is a daughter of the late Robert Megeath, widely known in this section.

Mr. Grehan by his sterling qualities of citizenship, high ideals of business ethics and the faithful discharge of his obligations to his county and state, had won the confidence and esteem of those with whom he was associated in social and business life.

He held membership in the following Masonic fraternities: Philomont Masonic Lodge, The Plains Royal Arch Chapter, The Plains Commandery and the Acca Shrine Temple at Richmond, Va.

He is survived by his widow, four children, two daughters and two sons, the eldest of which is ten years of age; two sisters, Mrs. Lawrence Beckley, New Jersey; Mrs. William Greenan, Alexandria, Va., and one brother, J. J. Grehan, Aldie, Virginia.

Funeral services were held from Mt. Zion Church on Wednesday of this week. Elder H. H. Lefferts officiating. Interment at Mt. Zion Church Cemetery.

The pallbearers were: Carroll F. Tyler, J. Marvin Leith, John M. Douglass, Harry E. Furr, Harry H. Riticor and Walter C. Ferguson.

LOUDOUN TIMES-MIRROR
Leesburg, Virginia
Thursday, February 9, 1928

DIES OF ACIDOSIS

Virginia Anne Thomas, age sixteen months, daughter of Mr. and Mrs. John G. Thomas of near Aldie, this county, died of acidosis at the Loudoun Hospital Sunday morning last. Funeral services were held Tuesday. Burial at Mt. Zion.

LOUDOUN TIMES-MIRROR
Leesburg, Virginia
April 5, 1928

MARRIED AT MT. ZION

The marriage rites for Mr. James I. Coffey of Washington and Mrs. Margaret C. Badger of Leesburg will be performed at Mt. Zion Baptist Church this afternoon at 5:00 o'clock, Elder H. H. Lefferts will officiate.

Mrs. Badger is the widow of the late Elder J. N. Badger of Aldie and Manassas and has a host of friends in this county.

LOUDOUN TIMES-MIRROR
Leesburg, Virginia
Thursday, November 1, 1928

ASSOCIATION AT MT. ZION

The Virginia Corresponding Meeting held its annual session with Mt. Zion Church October 17, 18, 19. There was a large crowd in attendance. Ministers and visitors from a distance were: Elders G. E. Coulborne, Cape Charles, Va,; L. H. Hardy, Atlantic, N. C.; J. T. Rowe, Baltimore, Md,; D. L. Topping, Baltimore, Md.; G. E. Ruston, New York; H. C. Kerr, Delmar, Del.; C. W. Vaughn, Hopewell, N. J.; T. W. Walker, Danville. All preached able sermons during the three days' meeting. Elder H. H. Lefferts, Moderator of the meeting also took part in the services. The next session will be held at Purcellville October 1929.

LOUDOUN TIMES-MIRROR
Leesburg, Virginia
Thursday, November 8, 1928

ARCOLA

Protracted services are in progress at this place with very good crowds in attendance each evening.

Among those from here who attended the Democratic speaking at Herndon Thursday evening last were Mr. and Mrs. A. L. Mankin and Mr. and Mrs. E. McFarland, all of whom enjoyed the remarks made by the various speakers. Yet none elicited more laughter or applause than the short talk by Mr. George Harrison of Herndon with his closing reference to the "bean beetle" and "Hoover Democrat."

Mr. and Mrs. William Whaley of Washington, were recent Arcola visitors. Mrs. Estelle Gaines and Miss Gaines of Leesburg, were Sunday afternoon callers at the home of Mrs. E. McFarland.

Two cars collided in front of C. A. Whaley's store Monday morning causing considerable damage to both cars though neither of the occupants was hurt. Mrs. S. J. Whaley and Miss Whaley are at Mr. C. A. Whaley's where they will spend the winter.

Mr. **Amos Johnson** of Little River, died at his home at that place Sunday night after an illness of some weeks. Burial at Mt. Zion on Tuesday.

LOUDOUN TIMES-MIRROR
Leesburg, Virginia
Thursday, November 15, 1928

MRS. FERGUSON SUCCUMBS

Mrs. **Mary C. Ferguson**, widow of the late Welton Ferguson of Arcola, died of pneumonia at Providence Hospital, October 30.

She is survived by a daughter, Miss Augie Ferguson of Falls Church with whom she made her home; two sons, Messrs Herbert and Raymond K. Ferguson of Washington and eight grandchildren.

Funeral services were held from the Falls Church Presbyterian Church and the body was interred by the side of her husband at Mt. Zion Friday, November 2.

LOUDOUN TIMES-MIRROR
Leesburg, Virginia
Thursday, November 15, 1928

DEATH OF AMOS JOHNSON

Mr. **William Amos Johnson** died November 4 after a lingering illness at his old home near Lenah. Surviving him are his widow, Mrs. Elizabeth Griffith Johnson; two sons, T. F. Johnson, Washington, D.C., W. G. Johnson, Norfolk, Va. and four daughters, Mrs. Evelyn Allison, Aldie, Va., Mrs. Emma Harrison, Washington, Mrs. Mary Lee, Beltsville, Md. and Miss Eula Johnson at home. He is also survived by sixteen grandchildren. Interment in Mt. Zion Cemetery on November 6.

LOUDOUN TIMES-MIRROR
Leesburg, Virginia
Thursday, November 22, 1928

ARCOLA

John Brent a colored resident of this community had the misfortune to be run down by a car driven by Mr. Robert Ellmore on Saturday last, sustaining a broken leg. The accident was considered unavoidable. Brent was removed at once to the Loudoun Hospital for surgical attention.

Mr. H. H. Palmer and Mrs. Palmer and family of Alexandria were Sunday guests of Mr. and Mrs. E. McFarland at their home 'Maxes Meadow.' Owing to the kindness and industry of some of the gentleman of the community the church in this place has been improved on the interior by two coats of paint. Not to be outdone in the good work the ladies of the church also did their part which can be attested to by the shining windows and polished door, all of which added to the recently installed Delco lights lends an added attractiveness to the surroundings. The Presiding Elder and the pastor, Rev. Mr. Wright were both present at the services on Sunday.

Mr. J. W. Marshall of Baltimore was an Arcola visitor on Saturday. **Richard Overhall** a worthy and respected colored man of this community died at his home near here one day last week aged ninety years. Interment at Mt. Zion.

Mr. Sidney Shears of Willard was the guest last week of his daughter and son-in-law, Mr. and Mrs. A. L. Mankin. Mr. and Mrs. Arthur Brown and daughter, Miss Rita, were also Sunday guests of Mr. and Mrs. Mankin. Mr. and Mrs. Crosen of Floris were Sunday visitors of their parents, Mr. and Mrs. Barb of this place.

Mr. D. C. Sands has improved his recently acquired property, formerly known as "The old race field," by the building of a handsome bungalow, barns and various outbuildings, fences, etc. Viewed from the highway one can imagine a little town sprung up in our midst which all goes to prove that Arcola has boomed at last. Mr. Richardson and family were Sunday visitors to Winchester.

LOUDOUN TIMES-MIRROR
Leesburg, Virginia
Thursday, December 20, 1928

EIGHTY YEARS YOUNG

Cherrydale, Va.--Friends and relatives brought their baskets to old Bull Run Farm on Thanksgiving Day and spread a feast there to honor the mistress of the home, Mrs. Sallie Thomas Carruthers. It was a happy birthday surprise and the immense cake bore eighty candles, marking the years of a long, useful and still active life.

There was appropriate music, several poems were read and short speeches made all suggestive of the lovely character known and felt by those who have come under her gentle influence. Her devotion to her church and all its people is known far and wide and the unbounded hospitality of her home and that of her late husband, Joel Carruthers, seem to say--"Let me live in my house by the side of the road, and be a friend to man."

COMMUNICATED

LOUDOUN TIMES-MIRROR
Leesburg, Virginia
Thursday, May 15, 1930

MRS. JOHN G. THOMAS DIES

Mrs. **Alice Pangle Thomas**, wife of Mr. John G. Thomas, of Lenah, Va., died Sunday, May 11, following an illness of three months. She was thirty-two years of age, and a member of the Arcola Methodist Church.

Mrs. Thomas is survived by her husband; a twenty-two months old son; one sister, Mrs. Leafy Linton, Clifton, Va., and one brother, Mr. Harry Pangle, of Arcola, Va.

Funeral rites were held from Mt. Zion Church Wednesday morning, Elder H. H. Lefferts officiating. Interment was made in Mt. Zion Cemetery.

LOUDOUN TIMES-MIRROR
Leesburg, Virginia
Thursday, July 3, 1930

MRS. SARAH CARRUTHERS DIES

Mrs. **Sarah Carruthers**, widow of Mr. Joel Carruthers, died Monday morning, June 30 at her home near Aldie, Va., following an attack of paralysis. She was 82 years of age and a daughter of the late Griffith Thomas and a native and life-long resident of the county.

Surviving her are four daughters, Mrs. Walter George, of Winchester; Mrs. Mae Thomas, Aldie; Mrs. Blanche Beasley, Norfolk, and Mrs. Robert Connor, of Clarendon, and one son, Mr. Elmer Carruthers of the University of Virginia.

Funeral services were held from Mount Zion Primitive Baptist Church Wednesday morning at 11:00 o'clock, Elder H. H. Lefferts officiating. Interment was in Mt. Zion Cemetery.

LOUDOUN TIMES-MIRROR
Leesburg, Virginia
Thursday, February 26, 1931

ESTEEMED COLORED WOMAN DIES

Lou Green, highly respected colored woman, died February 2 in the home of Miss R. L. Norman at Clarks Gap. Lou was 55 years old and had spent all of her life among "white folks." When an infant she was taken by Mrs. Clay Jenkins of Mount Gilead, who raised her. With the death of Mrs. Jenkins she went to live with Miss Norman.

More white persons than colored attended her funeral which was conducted by Elder Lefferts. Lou is survived by one son.

LOUDOUN TIMES-MIRROR
Leesburg, Virginia
Thursday, August 20, 1931

MRS. SUSANNAH T. MARSHALL

Mrs. **Susannah Turman Marshall,** 55, died at her home in Arcola August 11 after a long illness. She was a daughter of James M. and Tabitha Turman of Carroll County, Va. and the widow of I. Monroe Marshall who died June 3, 1897. Mrs. Marshall was a member of Mt. Zion Old School Baptist Church.

She is survived by two daughters, Mrs. Glennie Fleming, near Leesburg and Miss Virginia Alice Marshall at home; two sons, J. C. and E. F. Marshall, Arcola; one sister, Miss Alice Turman, Willis, Floyd County, Va. and four brothers, Dr. A. E. Turman, Dr. J. W. Turman, both of Richmond, Dr. O. F. Turman, Parksley, Va. and C. M. Turman, Arcola.

Funeral services were held at Mt. Zion Church by Elder H. H. Lefferts. Interment was made in the churchyard nearby.

[EDITOR'S NOTE: Mrs. Marshall was not a widow. Her husband, I. Monroe Marshall, died in 1953. The date June 3, 1897 is probably for their marriage.]

LOUDOUN TIMES-MIRROR
Leesburg, Virginia
Thursday, August 13, 1931

CLAN OF CARRUTHERS IN ANNUAL MEETING
Reunion of Society is Held in Mount Zion Church

The American Carruthers Clan Society held its annual meeting in Mount Zion Church, lower Loudoun, Sunday. Chieftain T. N. Carruthers presided. Members of the Clan, to the number of 60, attended.

Elmer I. Carruthers of the University of Virginia gave a history of the clan and a talk was made by Lester Bennett, while Mr. Adams of Washington gave humorous sketches and imitations.

Besides the members of the clan in Loudoun County, those present included Mrs. W. R. Floyd and W. F. Carruthers of Farmville, Va.; Mr. and Mrs. Walter George and daughter of Winchester, Mr. and Mrs. Lester Bennett, Miss Elizabeth Bennett and Miss Martha Bennett of Clarendon, Md. and Mrs. Robert Floyd and children, W. O. Carruthers, Mr. and Mrs. Charles Smith and two children, Miss Essie Lee Floyd, Miss Ida Gray Floyd, Miss Carrie Floyd, William Floyd, Mr. and Mrs. Virgil Williams and Mrs. Ollie Adams and sons of Washington, and Mr. and Mrs. Elmer I. Carruthers of Charlottesville.

Officers of the clan elected: Elmer I. Carruthers, deputy chieftain; Mrs. Virgil Williams, secretary; Miss Elizabeth Bennett, historian, and Mrs. Blanche Beasley, treasurer.

The Carruthers family came to this country in 1765 from Dumfries, Scotland, and settled in Cumberland County, Pa. Several branches of the family migrated to North Carolina and Tennessee and it is from these families that the present clan is descended.

LOUDOUN TIMES-MIRROR
Leesburg, Virginia
Thursday, February 23, 1933

MRS. CHARLES W. THOMAS

Mrs. **Rebecca May Thomas**, wife of Charles W. Thomas, died at her residence, "Bull Run," near Aldie February 16, following an illness of several weeks' duration. Mrs. Thomas was the daughter of the late Joel and Sarah F. Carruthers, and was 46 years of age. She was a devout member of the Aldie Methodist Episcopal Church, and for the past twenty years had served as president of the Ladies Aid Society of the church, and for several years past, a member of the Board of Stewards. She was a member of the Loudoun Chapter, U.D.C.

Mrs. Thomas enjoyed the esteem of a large circle of friends and relatives to whom she had endeared herself by many acts of kindness and love.

The funeral services were held at "Bull Run: by her pastor, the Rev. J. M. York, and were attended by a host of neighbors, relatives and friends, some of whom had traveled from distant points to pay the last rites to a loving friend.

Mrs. Thomas is survived by her husband, three sisters, Mrs. W. O. Beasley of Norfolk, Mrs. J. Robert Connor of Cherrydale and Mrs. W. B. George of Winchester, and one brother, Elmer I. Carruthers of the University of Virginia, all of whom were at her bedside when the end came.

The pallbearers, all cousins of the deceased, were Louie Thomas, Burns Seaton, Clarence R. Thomas, Thomas N. Carruthers, E. Lester Bennett, Dr. John G. Thomas, and Lorenzo Carruthers. Interment was in the family section of the Mt. Zion cemetery.

LOUDOUN TIMES-MIRROR
Leesburg, Virginia
Thursday, July 13, 1933

MRS. EMMA V. CRAIG

Mrs. Emma V. Craig, 86, widow of George W. Craig and lifelong resident of the Middleburg community, died Friday at the home of her grandson, Frank Craig, of Rochester, N.Y., where she has been visiting. She had been active and in good health all of her life until her recent illness which was only a few days duration. She was the daughter of the late John W. and Rachael Young Dodd, of Middleburg, and is the last member of her immediate family. She was one of the best known and highly esteemed residents of her community and for 45 years had been a member of the Old School Baptist Church.

She is survived by two grandsons, Frank S. Craig, Rochester, N.Y. and William T. Craig, Middleburg and a host of friends.

Funeral services were conducted from Mt. Zion Church Monday afternoon by Elder H. H. Lefferts. Burial was made in Sharon Cemetery, Middleburg.

Pallbearers were Frank Cole, Edward Norman, Newton Chamblin, Edwin Reamer, Frank Brittlebank and Baker Chamblin.

MRS. JAMES MARVIN LEITH

Mrs. James Marvin Leith, 67, died Saturday at her home in Aldie after a long illness. She was a daughter of the late Alfred and Mary Megeath.

She is survived by her husband, two brothers, A. P. Megeath and Herbert Megeath, three sisters, Mrs. John Ferguson, Herndon, Mrs. Johnson Furr and Mrs. James Ferguson of Aldie and a number of nieces and nephews, among whom is Mrs. Douglas Adams who made her home here.

Funeral services were held from the Methodist Church in Aldie and interment made in Sharon Cemetery, Middleburg.

39

LOUDOUN TIMES-MIRROR
Leesburg, Virginia
Thursday, August 24, 1933

MRS. LAURA M. SKINNER

Mrs. **Laura M. Skinner**, 76, died August 11 at her home near Aldie. She is survived by three children, John Lud and Robert Skinner of Aldie and Mrs. Roy G. Rhodes of Washington, D.C.; two sisters, Mrs. Westwood Hutchison, Manassas and Mrs. Mollie Ewell of Ruckersville. Burial was in Mt. Zion, the Rev. C. W. Trainham officiating.

LOUDOUN TIMES-MIRROR
Leesburg, Virginia
Thursday, September 28, 1933

RUTH EARL SKINNER

Ruth Earl, the two-year-old daughter of Mr. and Mrs. John L. **Skinner** of near Little River, died in the Loudoun County Hospital, September 22 from an attack of acidosis. The child was ill only a few hours.

Funeral services were conducted by the Revs. Long and Taylor and she was interred in Mt. Zion cemetery by the side of her grandmother who preceded her in death by only a few weeks.

LOUDOUN TIMES-MIRROR
Leesburg, Virginia
Thursday, October 12, 1933

LEFFERTS IS AGAIN CHOSEN MODERATOR
Leesburg Man Honored For 22nd Time By Old School Baptists

Elder H. H. Lefferts of Leesburg was yesterday re-elected for the twenty-first year in succession as moderator of the Virginia Corresponding Meeting of Old School Baptists, in session in the Mount Zion meeting house, near Aldie. G. C. Spindle of Washington was elected clerk. An attendance of 500 was registered for the opening session.

The introductory sermon was preached by Elder J. T. Rowe of Baltimore, Elder C. W. Vaughan of Hopewell, N.J., and Elder T. W. Walker of Danville, Va., preached during the afternoon.

Sermons today were delivered by Elder D. L. Topping of Baltimore, Elder G. H. Bellows of Roxbury, N.J., Elder H. C. Ker, Del Mar, Del.; and Elder Lefferts.

The Conference closes tomorrow with a conference of all ministers present. The Conference will meet next year in New Valley Church, Lucketts.

LOUDOUN TIMES-MIRROR
Leesburg, Virginia
Thursday, April 7, 1938

MRS. ROSE POWELL WATSON

Services will be held in Mt. Zion Old School Baptist Church, Friday at 2:00 o'clock for Mrs. **Rose Powell Watson**, 78, widow of Jacob B. Watson.

Mrs. Watson died Wednesday in the home of her daughter, Mrs. Ira Carter, in Aldie. She was the daughter of the late John and Harriett Everett and a lifelong resident of the county.

Besides her daughter she leaves one stepson, William Watson, New Haven, Conn.; three sisters, Mrs. John Thompson, Hamilton; Miss Maude Everett, Hamilton; Mrs. J. G. Carruthers, Round Hill and six grandchildren.

Services will be conducted by her pastor, Elder H. H. Lefferts and burial made in Mt. Zion Cemetery.

LOUDOUN TIMES MIRROR
Leesburg, Virginia
Thursday, October 19, 1939

WILLIAM JORDON

Funeral services were held Wednesday afternoon for **William Jordon** who died Monday morning at his home near Middleburg. Mr. Jordon, 52, suffered a heart attack Sunday night which caused his untimely death.

Mr. Jordon is survived by his wife, nee Miss Sadie Huff of Upperville and two daughters, Misses Marguerite and Memphis Jordon. He was a World War veteran and a member of the American Legion.

Services were conducted by the Rev. M. L. Ragland with interment in the family plot at Mt. Zion Church.

ALFRED P. MEGEATH, SR

Services were held from the Aldie Methodist Church on Saturday for Alfred P. Megeath, Sr., 69, who died late Thursday in the home of his daughter, Mrs. T. B. Hutchison, near Leesburg. Rites were conducted by the Rev. John Hendricks and burial made in Sharon Cemetery, Middleburg.

Pallbearers were Roy Hagenbuch, B. F. Fletcher, Drew Hutchison, Lacey Ferguson, Joe and Hasel Lacey.

Mr. Megeath while ill but two days had been in failing health since last August. He was a former deputy commissioner for Broad Run District and until retirement actively engaged in the farming industry. He was a son of the late Margaret and Alfred Megeath of the Aldie community and was widely known. He married Miss Olivia Leith who preceded him in death by three years to the date of his illness.

Besides Mrs. Hutchison, he leaves four other daughters, Mrs. J. Hildt Grubb, Purcellville; Mrs. Douglass Adams, Washington; Mrs. Fewell Melton, Haymarket, and Mrs. L. E. Thomas, Aldie; one son, Alfred P. Megeath, Jr., Aldie; two sisters, Mrs. Flora Ferguson and Mrs. Blanche Furr and one brother, Herbert Megeath, all of Aldie.

MRS. MAGNOLIA DANIEL

Mrs. **Magnolia Saffer Daniel**, 71, wife of John O. Daniel, a former delegate to the General Assembly of Virginia, died in her home near Leesburg, Thursday night after an illness of several weeks.

Mrs. Daniel was a daughter of the late Mr. and Mrs. Thornton Saffer of Aldie and in which community she spent her younger life. She is survived by her husband, two sons, Harry and John Daniel, Leesburg; two daughters, Mrs. W. W. Waters, Leesburg and Mrs. Rose Morris, Arlington; three sisters, Mrs. Lillie B. S. Grant, Mrs. Ocie Gibson, Fairfax and Mrs. Flora Gulick, Aldie; one brother, W. C. Saffer, Leesburg, and six grand children.

Funeral services were held Saturday afternoon, conducted by the Rev. D. C. Mayers of Middleburg. Interment was in Mt. Zion Cemetery. Pallbearers were Allen Gulick, Frank Riticor, Guy Mitchell, Austin, Clinton and Walton Saffer.

LOUDOUN TIMES-MIRROR
Leesburg, Virginia
Thursday, June 27, 1940

MRS. DORMAN HUTCHISON

The death early Sunday morning of Mrs. **Laura Smith Hutchison**, 76, wife of Dorman Hutchison of Lenah, was a distinct shock to her family and friends. Mrs. Hutchison was paralyzed Saturday night and never regained consciousness. She was a daughter of the late Henry and Elizabeth Riticor Smith of the Broad Run neighborhood and a lifelong member of Little River Baptist Church. Mrs. Hutchison was in Leesburg, Saturday, apparently recovered from an attack of illness in the late winter that had necessitated medical care.

She was widely known in Lower Loudoun and leaves a host of warm friends. Besides her husband, she is survived by one son, Carroll S. Hutchison; three daughters, Mrs. Roger Rusk, Ryan; Miss Blanche Hutchison at home, Miss Mary Hutchison, Washington and two brothers, Charles Smith, Baltimore, and William Smith, Lenah.

Funeral services were held from the home on Tuesday, the Rev. C. W. McElroy, her pastor, officiating. Burial was made in Mt. Zion Cemetery. Pallbearers were Milton Ish, John Lud Skinner, Gales Hutchison, Gus Hutchison, Robert Skinner and Tulous Costello.

LOUDOUN TIMES-MIRROR
Leesburg, Virginia
Thursday, November 28, 1940

MRS. ELLA BARTON

Mrs. **Ella Barton**, 70, a lifetime resident of Loudoun County, died November 22 at the home of her daughter, Mrs. S. O. Burton, at Lenah, after an illness of a year.

Mrs. Barton, the daughter of the late Kemp B. and Arbella Gochnaeur Furr, was born near Bluemont, April 18, 1870. She was married January 27, 1890 to Charles William Barton, a Confederate veteran, who died fourteen years ago. From this union three children were born. Charles B. Barton, of Arcola; Mrs. Stuart O. Burton, and Mrs. Carroll L. Flynn, of Lenah. She is also survived by her step-mother, Mrs. Margaret Furr of Mountville; four grandchildren, Mildred and Audrey Flynn, Margaret Ella and Everet Burton, of Lenah; six brothers; six sisters; and a number of nieces and nephews.

Mrs. Barton was a woman of noble character, and a church member since early childhood. Her patient spirit and kindly character endeared her to all who knew her.

Funeral services were held from the home of her daughter, Mrs. S. O. Burton, at Lenah, Sunday afternoon, the Rev. C. W. McElroy officiating. Interment was in Mt. Zion Cemetery, Aldie. Pallbearers were Charles Barton, Carroll Flynn, Stuart Burton, Carl, Warren and Walter Furr.

LOUDOUN TIMES-MIRROR
Leesburg, Virginia
Thursday, November 28, 1940

J. O. DANIEL RITES IN HOME YESTERDAY
Former Legislator Succumbs From
Heart Attack in Home of Daughter

The sudden passing on Monday afternoon of **John Orr Daniel**, retired merchant and former member of the House of Delegates from Loudoun brought profound sorrow to his many friends throughout the county and more particularly in the Evergreen Mills community where since boyhood he had made his home.

Mr. Daniel died from a heart attack in the home of his son-in-law and daughter, Mr. and Mrs. William Waters about 4 o'clock, Monday. Although he had been in declining health for several years or since a paralytic attack some months ago, his death came suddenly.

Mr. Daniel who was 77 represented his county in the State Legislature for twelve years, first sitting with the Virginia Assembly in 1906. There he served for a long period as chairman of the Committee on Roads and Navigation. He engaged in the Mercantile business at Evergreen Mills and at Watson during his early life at the same time operating his farm located in that section.

Few men were better known in the Evergreen Mills community than John Orr Daniel and few more popular. His kindnesses and keen sense of humor made for him many friends.

Mr. Daniel married Miss Magnolia Saffer who died March 28 of this year. He is survived by four children, J. W. Daniel, Harry C. Daniel and Mrs. Susie Waters, all of Evergreen Mills, Mrs. Rosa Morris of Washington and several grandchildren.

Last rites were conducted from his home near Leesburg Wednesday afternoon, Elder H. H. Lefferts officiating. Burial was made in Mt. Zion churchyard. Pallbearers were Joseph Shumate, Charles W. Atwell, Bernard Minor, Benjamin Fletcher, Henry Mitchell and W. C. Cooper.

MRS. GEORGIA M. ANDERSON

Mrs. **Georgia Matthew Anderson**, 79, died at her home near Catharpin, Monday. She was the wife of the late Ira Irmi Anderson, who died in 1934, and was a daughter of the late George and Abley (James) Matthew, of Loudoun County.

She leaves many relatives in Washington, Ohio and Virginia and is survived by two daughters and three sons: Mrs. Estelle Franklin, of Burkes Station; Mrs. Iva Matthew, of Manassas; Lester Anderson, of Catharpin; Lindon and Berkeley Anderson, of Washington; nine grandchildren and seven great-grandchildren.

She was a member of Mt. Zion Church and funeral services were held there on Thursday, Elder H. H. Lefferts officiating. Pallbearers were Emmit Pattie, Jett Pattie, Maurice Polen, Charles Johnson, Albert Ellison and Walter Allison.

MRS. MARGARET B. COFFEY

Many devoted friends gathered at historic Mt. Zion Old School Baptist Church near Aldie on Sunday afternoon to pay last tribute to Mrs. **Margaret Badger Coffey**, who passed away on Friday in the home of Mr. and Mrs. John G. Thomas, where she made her home for the past four years. Rites were conducted by her pastor, Elder H. H. Lefferts and burial was made in Mt. Zion Church Cemetery by the the side of her first husband, Elder J. N. Badger. Pallbearers were C. M. Turman, J. S. Gulick, C. G. Spindle, Edwin Reamer, J. G. and C. W. Thomas.

Mrs. Coffey was born in Fauquier County, April 16, 1855, the daughter of Thomas and Jane Carrington Hunton, and is the last member of a family of three brothers and three sisters. In 1885 she was married to the late Elder J. N. Badger, of Aldie, and with him made her home in Aldie and later at Manassas. Elder Badger died in December, 1914. In April, 1928, she was married to James I. Coffey, of Washington, who passed away September, 1937. As Mrs. Badger, she made her home at one time in Leesburg, where she is well known by older friends. Surviving are a niece, Miss Margaret Cox, and a nephew, Hunton Cox, both of Washington.

LOUDOUN TIMES-MIRROR
Leesburg, Virginia
Thursday, October 21, 1943

ABRAHAM C. PHILLIPS

Abraham Colon Phillips, 31, son of Posy Franklin Phillips, near Leesburg, and the late Mrs. Bertie Sutphin Phillips, died in the home of his father on Monday after illness of several months. He had been a resident of Loudoun for twenty-five years, moving here with his father from Floyd County. Young Phillips was a native of Indian Valley, Va. and was unmarried.

Besides his father and step-mother, he leaves a sister, Mrs. Frankie Hawes, Baltimore; a half brother and five half-sisters. Funeral services were held Wednesday from Slack's Funeral Home Elder H. H. Lefferts officiating. Burial was made in the family plot beside his mother in Mt. Zion Cemetery.

LOUDOUN TIMES-MIRROR
Leesburg, Virginia
September 16, 1948

MRS. IDA C. PRESGRAVES

Graveside services were held in Mount Zion Cemetery, near Aldie, for Mrs. **Ida C. Presgraves**, 91 of Washington, who was burned to death on Thursday in a fire in a Travilah, Md. boarding house. Rites were conducted by Elder H. H. Lefferts, of Leesburg.

A native of Loudoun, Mrs. Presgraves was the wife of Eugene W. Presgraves, a merchant in Lenah, who died 20 years ago. She was a member of Mount Zion Old School Baptist Church. Survivors included a daughter, Mrs. May L. Isbell, and a grandchild, both of Washington.

LOUDOUN TIMES-MIRROR
Leesburg, Virginia
Thursday, April 28, 1949

CLAUDIUS T. HIXSON

Claudius Theodore Hixson, 69, died unexpectly on Monday at his farm in the Hamilton section. A lifelong resident of the county, he was a son of the late Nelson Hixson. Mr. Hixson was a regular attendant at Mt. Zion Old School Baptist Church. He had a wide circle of friends.

Besides his wife, Mrs. Betty Thomas Hixson, he is survived by three sisters, Mrs. Mazie Lowe, Martinsburg, W. Va.; Mrs. Mary Hammett and Mrs. Lydia Bondurant, both of Farmville, Va.

Funeral services were held from Mt. Zion Old School Baptist Church on Wednesday by Elder H. H. Lefferts. Interment was made in the church cemetery.

The pallbearers were Wade Geiman, Clarence W. Hall, Samuel Welsh, Nathan Lowry, J. M. Cole and Ray Hawling.

LOUDOUN TIMES-MIRROR
Leesburg, Virginia
Thursday, May 25, 1950

MRS. ELIZABETH JOHNSON

Mrs. **Elizabeth Johnson**, 93, wife of the late William Amos Johnson, died in the home of her daughter, Mrs. Charles B. Barton, near Aldie, on May 18, after an illness of ten weeks.

Mrs. Johnson was born in Prince William County, a daughter of the late Harriet and William Griffith. In young womanhood she moved into the Little River neighborhood, where she lived most of her life and where she endeared herself to her neighbors and friends through her kindness.

Mrs. Johnson was a member of Little River Baptist Church for a number of years and until her health failed she was a faithful attendant of her church. About ten years ago she moved to Arcola to be with her daughter.

Besides Mrs. Barton, she is survived by the following children: Mrs. Robert Allison, Lenah; Mrs. Ashby Harrison, Arcola; Mrs. Frank Lee, Beltsville, Md.; Trollus Johnson, Aldie and Grafton Johnson, Washington. Also surviving are 16 grand children, 34 great grand children and two great great grandchildren.

Funeral services were conducted by the Rev. Warren Lee Oliff, pastor of Little River Baptist Church, and the Rev. Mr. Fowler, pastor of Mt. Hope Baptist Church in Royston Funeral Home, Middleburg. She was laid to rest in Mt. Zion Cemetery by the side of her husband.

The pallbearers were C. C. Flynn, C. W. Whaley, Fern Marshall, J. W. Mitchell, W. T. Costello and John Ludd Skinner.

LOUDOUN TIMES-MIRROR
Leesburg, Virginia
Thursday, May 3, 1951

3 REASONS FOR ALDIE'S HOPES
Slim Edwards   Bud Kirk   Guy Jackson

Above are three key additions to the Aldie team of 1951, snapped after they had dressed on the completion of a stiff workout on the diamond. From left to right are Slim Edwards crack pitcher, Bud Kirk long distant clouter, who will hold down first base, and Guy Jackson, former Aldie ace but who for the past several seasons has starred for Purcellville teams and who is expected to fill the hole at the hot corner.

Stout Skinny Jackson, co-manager of the Aldie team, was sunning himself on the bench during a workout of the club. "We're all right," he said. "As a matter of fact, we're a little better off than last year when we moved out of the cellar for the first time in years. Our pitching with Slim Edwards on hand figures to rate with the league's best. Remember we have Philyaw, Mutt Edwards, Trenary and Bettis to back up Slim.

You may not believe it, but Bud Kirk is showing the old college spirit and hitting well. Rattler Leith seems to be getting younger as the years go by. Guy is going to help us tremendously at third base and Young Tommy Saffer is going to surprise a lot of people. Our outfield is well taken care of by Peacemaker, Dick Edwards, McIntosh and Waddell.

And don't forget that my co-manager Cooley Edwards, a fine backstop, with plenty of life, will be in there too. We also have capable reserves. I think we have a winner this year and the fans of the community think so too. They sense victory."

48

LOUDOUN TIMES-MIRROR
Leesburg, Virginia
Thursday, June 21, 1951

THOMAS FAMILY HOLDS ITS 18TH ANNUAL REUNION

The Griffith Thomas family held its eighteenth annual reunion on Sunday, with an attendance of approximately 100. The all-day picnic took place on the grounds of Mt. Zion Church, which this year is celebrating its one hundredth anniversary.

Those from a distance attending the reunion were Walter E. Thomas, Raleigh, N. C.; Mr. and Mrs. Orien Mellott, son-in-law and daughter, all from McConnellsburg, Pa.; Mr. and Mrs. C. R. Thomas and Miss Elizabeth Allen, of Charlottesville; Mr. and Mrs. James Edward Miller and two sons, of Fort Knox, Ky.; Mr. and Mrs. S. F. Ellington and son, of Waynesboro; Elder and Mrs. J. D. Wood, of Roanoke; Mr. and Mrs. Elmer Schooley, of McConnellsburg, Pa.

After a picnic lunch, the business meeting was called by the retiring president, C. W. Thomas. Officers elected for two years are Elmer Thomas, president; Shirley Thomas, vice-president and Miss Claudie Thomas, secretary-treasurer.

A gift was presented to Mrs. Betty Thomas Hixson, eldest member of the family present.

LOUDOUN TIMES-MIRROR
Leesburg, Virginia
Thursday, August 30, 1951

DR. JOHN G. THOMAS

Funeral services for Dr. **John G. Thomas**, 67, retired veterinarian and former deputy sheriff of Loudoun were held from Mount Zion Old School Baptist Church on Sunday. Elder J. E. Wood conducted the services. Burial was made in the churchyard.

The pallbearers were Roger Powell, Wilmer Cross, Ralph Styer, John Pollard, Jesse Frame and Curtis Ambler.

Dr. Thomas died in Loudoun Hospital on Thursday, after a brief illness. He had, however, been in failing health for several years. He was a son of William Phineas and Sallie Riticar Thomas, and was born near Aldie. Dr. Thomas spent his entire life in the section in which he died. He served as deputy sheriff for five years, retiring because of ill health. He was a member of Mount Zion Old School Baptist Church.

Dr. Thomas is survived by his widow, Mrs. Gertrude Rusk Thomas; a son, Pfc. Earl Griffith Thomas, stationed at Fort Belvoir; three sisters, Mrs. David Farnie, Leesburg; Mrs. Orien Mellott of Penn, and Mrs. Margaret Ellington, Waynesboro, Va., and three brothers, Henry P. Thomas, Alexandria; Clarence R. Thomas, Charlottesville, and Charles W. Thomas, Philomont.

LOUDOUN TIMES-MIRROR
Leesburg, Virginia
Thursday, July 12, 1951

OLD SCHOOL BAPTIST CHURCH HERE
TO MARK 100TH ANNIVERSARY

Members of Mt. Zion Old School Baptist Church, on Route 50, near Gilbert's Corner are making preparation to observe, on July 22 the one hundredth anniversary of its present meeting house. The church was organized in 1850 with 14 members, including the following names: Lee, Ish, Marshall, Hutchison, Gulick, Rogers, Horsman, Foley, Matthew, Mattose and Lynn. Elder Robert C. Leachman was the first pastor. Their faith and order was, still remains, the same as the ancient Baptist Church, and they are sometimes distinguished as Predestinarian Baptists.

In addition to Elder Leachman, the following Elders have served as pastors of Mt. Zion: J. L. Perrington, J. N. Badger and H. H. Lefferts, with J. D. Wood serving at the present time.

There are numerous descendants of the founders living in this and adjoining counties and each year they assemble for a memorial meeting for those buried in the cemetery.

An all-day meeting is planned for the fourth Sunday in July, at which time a short history of the church will be given by the pastor and an address will be delivered by Henry P. Thomas. Preaching services will be held in the morning and afternoon by Elder C. E. Turner, and the pastor, Elder J. D. Wood. The public will be welcome at the service.

LOUDOUN TIMES-MIRROR
Leesburg, Virginia
Thursday, July 26, 1951

OLD SCHOOL BAPTISTS OBSERVE ANNIVERSARY

The hundredth anniversary of Mt. Zion Old School Baptist Church was observed on Sunday with an all-day meeting and picnic lunch. Many people came from various parts of the country for the occasion.

Ministers taking part in the celebration were Elder George Weaver, of Huntington, W. Va., Elder C. E. Turner, of Martinsburg, Va., and the pastor, Elder J. D. Wood, who read the constitution, decorum and history of the church was formed a century ago and compiled by Elder Wood and the church clerk, Mrs. Mabel Thomas Farnie, from the minutes of the church.

An address by Henry P. Thomas, of Alexandria, a grandson of one of the signers of the deed of the church in 1851, concluded the celebration.

50

LOUDOUN TIMES-MIRROR
Leesburg, Virginia
Thursday Afternoon, January 24, 1952

EDWARD D. HUTCHISON DIES IN LENAH HOME

Funeral services were held Sunday from Little River Baptist Church for **Edward Dorman Hutchison**, 88, widely known resident of the Broad Run section of Loudoun. His pastor, the Rev. Warren Lee Oliff, conducted the rites. Burial was made in Mt. Zion Church Cemetery nearby.

The pallbearers were T. Gales Hutchison, Tulloss Costello, Robert Skinner, Milton Ish, B. B. Hutchison, and John L. Skinner.

Mr. Hutchison, retired farmer, died in his home, near Lenah, last Thursday. He was the husband of the late Laura Smith Hutchison, whose death occurred 13 years ago.

Mr. Hutchison was a lifetime resident of Loudoun, a progressive farmer and a popular citizen. He was an active churchman and civic leader. A host of friends from throughout this and adjoining counties gathered to pay him final tribute.

Surviving is one son, Carroll S. Hutchison, Aldie and three daughters, Mrs. R. E. Rusk, Ashburn; Miss Blanche Hutchison, at home, and Mrs. Milton A. Lehr, Washington.

LOUDOUN TIMES-MIRROR
Leesburg, Virginia
Thursday Afternoon, July 3, 1952

MRS. ROBERT L. ALLISON

Mrs. **Evelyn Gaynell Allison**, 66, wife of Robert L. Allison, and daughter of the late William Amos and Elizabeth Griffith Johnson, died in her home at Lenah on June 27.

Mrs. Allison was an active member of Little River Baptist Church until the past few years when her health prohibited her attendance. She was devoted to her family and was regarded as a good neighbor to all.

Mrs. Allison is survived by her husband, a daughter, Mrs. Edward O. Carroll, Catharpin, and a granddaughter whom she reared, Mrs. George Rollison, Waterford. Also, surviving are thirteen grandchildren, three great grandchildren; three sisters, Mrs. Emma Harrison, Mrs. Mary Lee and Mrs. Eula Barton; two brothers, Troylus and Grafton Johnson.

Funeral services were held Monday from Royston Funeral Home, Middleburg, conducted by the Rev. Warren Lee Oliff, pastor of Little River Baptist Church. Interment was made in Mt. Zion Cemetery, Aldie. The pallbearers were Gales Hutchison, Robert Skinner, W. T. Costello, Carroll Flynn and Charles Barton.

LOUDOUN TIMES-MIRROR
Leesburg, Virginia
Thursday Afternoon, March 26, 1953

MONROE MARSHALL FUNERAL AT ARCOLA

Funeral services were held from Mt. Zion Old School Baptist Church on Wednesday for **Isaac Monroe Marshall**, 79, who died Monday in the home of his son, E. F. Marshall near Arcola. The Rev. John Wood, pastor of the church, conducted the rites. Burial was made in Mt. Zion churchyard.

The pallbearers were Jay, Phil and William Marshall, Thomas and Marshall Fleming and Don Middleton.

Mr. Marshall, native of Carroll County, Va., had lived in Loudoun for 40 years. He had owned and operated a farm in the Arcola section until six years ago when he sold his property and went to make his home with his son. He was a regular attendant at services in Mt. Zion Church. Mr. Marshall was widely known to the people of his community and was regarded as a fine citizen and a friend to many.

Surviving are three children, E. F. Marshall, Arcola, with whom he lived; Mrs. C. P. Fleming, Leesburg and Mrs. Withers Murphy, Culpeper. Also surviving are ten grandchildren.

LOUDOUN TIMES-MIRROR
Leesburg, Virginia
Thursday, August 5, 1954

MRS. HIXSON, 92 OBSERVES BIRTHDAY

Mrs. Betty Hixson celebrated her ninety-second birthday on Sunday (August 1) in the home of Mrs. Veda Lee Lacey and Mr. and Mrs. Berkley Lee near Leesburg.

Mrs. Hixson received a number of gifts, cards and enjoyed a pleasant time, with refreshments served at conclusion of the party.

Among the guests present were Mr. and Mrs. Arch Donohoe and granddaughter, Mary Ann Donohoe, of California; Mrs. and Mrs. Robert Connor and cousin Marjory Bennett, of Syracuse, N.Y.; Mr. and Mrs. David Farnie, Mr. and Mrs. Otho Daniel, Mrs. George Moss, Leesburg; Louie Thomas, of Haymarket; Henry Alexander Thomas, of Alexandria, and Mr. and Mrs. Claude Thomas, of Hamilton.

LOUDOUN TIMES-MIRROR
Leesburg, Virginia
Thursday, November 18, 1954

MRS. L. V. BOLT FUNERAL HELD FROM MT. ZION

The funeral for Mrs. **Lillie V. Bolt**, 81, mother of Mrs. Ocie Dickens, of Leesburg, was held from Mt. Zion Old School Baptist Church, conducted by Elder W. G. Fletcher, of Strasburg. Burial was made in Mt. Zion Cemetery, near Aldie.

The pallbearers were Chester Sorratt, Staunton; Luther and Melvin Bolt, Falls Church; Edgar Dickens, Leesburg; Charles Bolt, Alexandria and Billy Bolt, of Bristo, Va.

Mrs. Bolt died in the home of a son, K. C. Bolt, near Bristo, Va. on November 2. She was born in Carroll County, Virginia but had lived in Loudoun greater part of the time since 1927. For the past eight years she has lived with her children. She was the widow of Thomas J. Bolt and was the mother of ten children. Her two eldest sons, C. Brown and Cecil C. Bolt, preceded her in death.

Surviving are four sons and four daughters, K. C. Bolt, near Bristo, Va.; Charles C., Jerome, Va.; Obie B., Harpers Ferry; John F., Annandale; Mrs. Claudie Sorratt, Staunton; Mrs. Ocie Dickens, Leesburg; Mrs. Alma Norby, Keene, Va. and Miss Charity Dickens, Silver Hill. Also she leaves several grandchildren and great grandchildren.

LOUDOUN TIMES-MIRROR
Leesburg, Virginia
Thursday, January 26, 1956

FUNERAL FRIDAY FOR MRS. HIXSON

Funeral services for Mrs. **Betty Thomas Hixson**, 93, widow of Claude T. Hixson, will be held from Mt. Zion Old School Baptist Church in Loudoun County at 11 o'clock, Friday (January 27), Elder J. D. Wood, pastor of Mt. Zion Church, will officiate at the service. Burial will be made in Mt. Zion churchyard.

Mrs. Hixson died in Clopton Nursing Home Tuesday night after a long period of invalidism.

Mrs. Hixson is a daughter of the late Griffith I. and Rebecca B. Thomas and is a lifelong resident of Loudoun. She was born in the county August 1, 1862 and had lived on the family farm in the Woodburn section until her husband's death seven years ago.

Mrs. Hixson was a regular attendant at Mt. Zion Old School Baptist Church and until the past two years was present at all of the Griffith Thomas family reunions. She was the great aunt of members of the Thomas family in Loudoun and was greatly beloved by many.

Nieces and nephews are her closest survivors, among them Mrs. David Farnie, of Leesburg.

LOUDOUN TIMES-MIRROR
Leesburg, Virginia
Thursday, August 23, 1956

T. F. JOHNSON 63, SUCCUMBS IN HOSPITAL

Troylous Franklin Johnson, 63, died August 19 in Loudoun Hospital. He was born near Lenah, a son of the late Amos and Elizabeth Griffith Johnson.

Mr. Johnson was the husband of Carrie Virginia Johnson and father of Mrs. Ruby East, of Landover, Md.; Mrs. Catherine Rollins, Bradbury Heights; Mrs. Lewis Herwitt, Fairfax; Mrs. Irene Myers, Long Beach, Cal.; Mrs. Norma Grimes, Arcola. Also he leaves two sons, William H. Johnson, Warrenton; John A. Johnson, Aldie and three sisters, Mrs. Ashby Harrison, Herndon; Mrs. Frank Lee, Beltsville, Md.;, and Mrs. Charlie Barton, Aldie.

LOUDOUN TIMES-MIRROR
Leesburg, Virginia
Thursday, August 15, 1957

MR. SHOCKLEY'S FUNERAL ON SATURDAY

Jay C. Shockley, Arcola merchant, 64, died in Loudoun Hospital on August 13 after illness of six weeks. Mr. Shockley had lived in lower Loudoun for more than 50 years and was well known to many of the people in that section.

Besides his wife, Rachel Downs Shockley, he leaves two daughters, Miss Marian Rachel Shockley, Arcola and Miss Mary Virginia Shockley, Falls Church; one sister, Mrs. Berkley Poland, Sterling, and one brother, James Shockley, Stephens City, Va.

Mr. Shockley was born in Hillsville, Va. He attended Old School Baptist Church and for 26 years was a member of the Southern States Cooperative.

Funeral services will be held Saturday at 2 p.m. from Arcola Methodist Church, the Rev. E. R. Thayer and the Rev. Willie Davis officiating. Interment will be made in Mt. Zion Cemetery.

The active pallbearers will be Robert Cornelius, Lester Pangle, Brooke Grimes, Roger Rusk, Roger Jenkins and James Kirkpatrick.

Honorary pallbearers will be Fern Marshall, Benjamin Hutchison, Carroll Hutchison, Carroll Downs, Mason Downs and John Minor.

LOUDOUN TIMES-MIRROR
Leesburg, Virginia
Thursday, April 14, 1960

ROBERT ALLISON, LIVED AT LENAH

Robert L. Allison, 74, farmer, and a former resident of Lenah, died April 5 in Blue Ridge Sanitorium where he had been under medical treatment for a number of years.

Surviving is one daughter, Mrs. E. O. Carroll of Falls Church, 13 grandchildren and seven great grandchildren. He leaves two sisters, Mrs. Lula McDaniel, Vienna and Mrs. John Donovan of Bristow, Va.

Funeral services were held in Royston's funeral home on Saturday conducted by the Rev. James Smith, pastor of Little River Baptist Church. Burial was in the family plot in Mt. Zion churchyard.

LOUDOUN TIMES-MIRROR
Leesburg, Virginia
Thursday, April 13, 1961

C. W. THOMAS 80, NATIVE OF LOUDOUN

Charles W. Thomas died suddenly from a heart seizure on April 5 in the home of his cousin, Mrs. B. B. Hutchison of Arcola.

Mr. Thomas was the son of William Phineas and Sally Riticor Thomas. He was born and lived his entire 80 years in Loudoun. He had been a farmer until a few years ago. After the death of his wife, Mabel Furr Thomas, he retired and lived in and near Leesburg.

Surviving are his three children by a former marriage, Mrs. Stuart Barrett of Alexandria, J. Rector Thomas of Arlington and Julia Sowers of Aldie; two sisters Mrs. Margaret Ellington of Waynesboro and Mrs. Mabel Farnie of Leesburg, two brothers Clarence Thomas of Charlottesville and Henry P. Thomas of Alexandria.

Funeral services were held Saturday from Mt. Zion Old School Baptist Church with burial in the adjoining cemetery. Elder John D. Wood of Manassas conducted the services.

THE LOUDOUN TIMES-MIRROR
Leesburg, Virginia
Thursday, January 14, 1965

CARROLL S. HUTCHISON, 67, WAS ONCE DEPUTY SHERIFF

Carroll Smith Hutchison, 67, died at his home at Lenah on Jan. 8 from a heart seizure. A former deputy sheriff for Loudoun, he had been in ill health for a number of years.

Mr. Hutchison spent his lifetime in Broad Run District. He was a son of the late Edward Dorman and Laura Smith Hutchison whose home also was at Lenah.

He was educated in the public schools of Loudoun and afterwards joined the State Police Force in which work he engaged for some time. He later worked for the Sheriff's Department in Loudoun and was serving as deputy at time of his retirement. Mr. Hutchison also had operated a grain mill at Lenah. He was a member of Little River Baptist Church.

Surviving are his wife, Mrs. Daisy Johnson Hutchison and three sisters, Mrs. Ruth Rusk and Miss Blanche B. Hutchison, both of Aldie and Mrs. Mary Lehr of Washington.

Funeral services were held Sunday afternoon from Royston's Chapel in Middleburg, conducted by the Rev. James Smith, pastor of Little River Baptist Church. Burial was in the family plot in Mt. Zion Old School Baptist Cemetery.

The pallbearers were Robert Skinner, John Skinner, Paul Adams, Jack Hutchison, Stanley E. Wilson and Paul Alexander.

LOUDOUN TIMES-MIRROR
Leesburg, Virginia
Thursday, August 5, 1965

JAS. CONNOR, WAS NATIVE OF LOUDOUN

James Robert Connor, 75, a retired government employee, died July 20 at his Arlington residence following a long illness. He had lived in the same house for 39 years.

Mr. Connor was born in Loudoun and on Dec. 8, 1923 he was married to Lelia Carruthers in Aldie. They moved to Arlington in 1926 when Mr. Connor began his career in the construction business. He had been employed with the General Services Administration for 20 years at the time of his retirement in 1960.

He was a member of St. Andrews Episcopal Church, Arlington. Besides his widow, he leaves a sister, Mrs. Mary C. Adams, 1811 N. Kenmore St., Arlington, and several nieces and nephews.

Services were held at Ives Funeral Home on July 23 with burial in Mount Zion Church Cemetery, Aldie.

LOUDOUN TIMES-MIRROR
Leesburg, Virginia
Thursday, March 9, 1967

MRS. SHOCKLEY, ONCE OF ARCOLA

Mrs. **Lucie Mae Shockley**, 66, wife of James M. Shockley, and at one time a resident of Arcola, died Feb. 25. The home was at White Post, Va.

Funeral services were held Tuesday from the Muse and Reed Chapel at Leesburg conducted by Elder John D. Wood of the Old School Baptist Church. Burial was in Mt. Zion Church Cemetery near Aldie.

Besides her husband, Mrs. Shockley is survived by three daughters and two sons, Mrs. George Pearson of Aldie, Mrs. Roy Lemon of Falls Church and Miss Lucie Mae Shockley of White Post, James M. Shockley of Front Royal and Sterling N. Shockley of Winchester and nine grandchildren and one great-grandson.

The pallbearers were Raymond and Paul Downs, John and Sam Nalls, Gorley Gregg and John W. Weimer.

LOUDOUN TIMES-MIRROR
Leesburg, Virginia
Thursday, November 6, 1969

CHARLES BARTON, 75, OF CHANTILLY

Charles Broadway Barton, 75, a retired carpenter, died Monday in Loudoun Memorial Hospital. He lived at Chantilly. Mr. Barton was a son of the late Charles William and Ella Furr Barton and was a member of Mt. Hope Baptist Church at Ashburn. Surviving are his wife, Eula Johnson Barton, and two sisters, Mrs. S. O. Burton and Mrs. Carroll Flynn, both of Aldie. Funeral services will be at 11 a.m. today (Thursday) at the Royston Funeral Home in Middleburg followed by burial in Mt. Zion Cemetery, Aldie. The Rev. John Gindlesperger, pastor of Mt. Hope, will conduct the services. The pallbearers are Julian Fouche, Gus Caylor, Stanley Wortman, Keith and Kenneth Gardner, and Gerald Smith.

LOUDOUN TIMES-MIRROR
Leesburg, Virginia
Thursday, May 29, 1969

HENRY P. THOMAS, 75 WAS LOUDOUN NATIVE

Henry P. Thomas, 75, past president of the board of directors of an Alexandria savings and loan association and a Loudoun native, died May 23 in Alexandria Hospital after an apparent heart attack. His home was in Alexandria.

A lawyer, Mr. Thomas was a 30-year member of the board of Security Savings and Loan Association and was made its honorary chairman in 1966.

He was a member of the Lincoln graduating class of 1912 and as an alumnus of the school, he presented annually the Henry P. Thomas award to the senior showing the greatest all-around improvement. He likewise was generous in his gifts to the present Lincoln elementary school and was the instigator of numerous alumni gatherings at Lincoln.

Mr. Thomas attended the University of Virginia and obtained his LLB and LLM degrees from the old National University School of Law in Washington. He observed the Navy for three years during World War I.

He formed his own law firm in 1924 and became active in numerous civic affairs. In 1952, he was appointed Virginia commissioner on the National Conference of Commissioners on Uniform State Law, and in 1962, he became a life member of the group.

Mr. Thomas was also a member of the American, D.C. and Virginia bar associations and was past president of the Alexandria Bar Association. He served on the board of Security National Bank at Baileys Crossroads from its organization in 1960.

He was a regent for Gunston Hall and was active in the restoration of Gadsby's Tavern. He was a past president of the Alexandria Optimists Club and a member of the University Club of Washington, the Jefferson Island Club and the American Legion.

He leaves his wife, the former Jane Colton; two sons, Henry Alexander and William Griffith, both of Alexandria; a sister, Mrs. Margaret Ellington of Waynesboro, and five grandchildren.

Burial was Monday in Mount Zion Church Cemetery near Aldie following services at St. Paul's Episcopal Church, Alexandria. The family requests that expressions of sympathy be in the form of contributions to the Heart Fund or to Alexandria Hospital.

LOUDOUN TIMES-MIRROR
Leesburg, Virginia
Thursday, February 19, 1970

MR. SHOCKLEY, RETIRED FARMER

James M. Shockley, a retired Loudoun County farmer, died Feb. 10 in Warren County Hospital, Front Royal. He was 71.

A former resident of the Arcola area of Loudoun, Mr. Shockley was born in Carroll County, Va., and had recently lived in Front Royal with a son, James M. Shockley, Jr. He was a son of the late Canada and Mary Huff Shockley.

Surviving with the son in Front Royal are another son, Sterling M. Shockley of Winchester; three daughters, Mrs. Robert Canard of Middleburg, Mrs. Roy Lemon of Falls Church and Miss Lucy Shockley, also of Falls Church; a sister, Mrs. Berkley Poland of Chantilly; nine grandchildren and three great-grandchildren.

Funeral services were held Feb. 13 at the Muse and Reed Funeral Home, Leesburg with interment in Mt. Zion Cemetery near Aldie. Elder John Wood officiated at the services.

LOUDOUN TIMES-MIRROR
Leesburg, Virginia
Thursday, August 20, 1970

JOHNSON RITES HELD IN LEESBURG

Carrie V. Johnson, 78, of Aldie, died Aug. 14 in George Washington University Hospital, Washington, D.C. She was the widow of Troylous Johnson.

Funeral services were held Tuesday at the Muse and Reed Funeral Home in Leesburg with interment in Mt. Zion Cemetery, Aldie. The Rev. John Gindlesperger, pastor of Calvary Baptist Church, officiated.

Mrs. Johnson is survived by five daughters, Mrs. Ruby East of Oxon Hill, Md., Mrs. Catherine Rollins of Bradbury Heights, Md., Mrs. Louise Hewitt of Fairfax, Mrs. Irene Myers of Long Beach, Calif., and Mrs. Norma Grimes of Arcola; two sons, William H., of Warrenton and John A. of Aldie; a sister, Mrs. Mary Ketland of Washington, D.C.; three brothers, B. Frank, Charles and David C. Lee, all of Beltsville, Md.; 16 grandchildren and 11 great-grandchildren.

The pallbearers were William Johnson Jr., Robert and Donnie Johnson, Lewis East Jr., Robert Lee, and Cecil Bryant.

LOUDOUN TIMES-MIRROR
Leesburg, Virginia
Thursday, February 18, 1971

ROY B. JENKINS, COUNTY NATIVE

Roy B. Jenkins, 79, a native of Loudoun County and a retired sergeant with the U. S. Park Police, died Feb. 10 in Suburban Hospital, Bethesda, Md. He lived at 4417 River Road, N.W., Washington.

Born on Mt. Gilead, the son of Clay and Emma Jenkins, Mr. Jenkins spent his youth in Loudoun and served in the U.S. Army during World War I. After the war, he moved to Washington and spent the remainder of his life there.

Active in the Masons, he was a past master of George C. Whitney Lodge in Georgetown and a past patron of Mizpah Chapter No. 8, Order of the Eastern Star, also in Georgetown.

He leaves his wife, Helen A. Jenkins, of the home address, and a son, Maj. Elmer Jenkins, U.S. Army Ret.

Funeral services were held Monday in Washington with burial in the family plot in Mt. Zion Cemetery at Aldie.

LOUDOUN TIMES-MIRROR
Leesburg, Virginia
Thursday, March 8, 1973

B. HUTCHINSON

Miss **Blanche B. Hutchison**, 69, of Aldie, died Mar. 4 in Loudoun Memorial Hospital. She was a retired school teacher, having taught in Loudoun County schools for 47 years.

Miss Hutchison retired from the teaching profession from Aldie Elementary School, after teaching in many Loudoun schools, including Middleburg, Arcola, Pleasant Valley, and earlier one-room schools.

The daughter of the late E. Dorman and Laura Smith Hutchison, Miss Hutchison was born at Hickory Grove, Prince William County. Later she moved with her parents to Lenah where she spent the remainder of her life.

Miss Hutchison was educated at Madison College, Harrisonburg, and the University of Virginia at Charlottesville. She was a member of the Aldie Presbyterian Church.

Surviving are two sisters, Mrs. Ruth E. Rusk of Aldie and Mrs. Mary H. Lehr of Washington, D.C.; and a nephew, Roger E. Rusk, Jr. of Washington.

Funeral services were conducted Mar. 7 at the Royston Funeral Home, Middleburg, with Chaplain Goetz of the Military District of Washington, D.C. officiating. Interment was in Mt. Zion Cemetery, near Aldie.

LOUDOUN TIMES-MIRROR
Leesburg, Virginia
Thursday, September 20, 1973

PAMELIA SKINNER

Mrs. **Pamelia Ish Skinner**, 85, wife of John Lud Skinner of Aldie, died in a Leesburg nursing home Sept. 13 after a long illness.

Mrs. Skinner was a retired school teacher and had taught both before and after her marriage. Her parents were the late Edgar and Pamelia Lynn Ish of the Aldie area. Until her illness Mrs. Skinner had been an active member of Little River Baptist Church, and in other years had taught Sunday School there.

Besides her husband, she is survived by a son, James Milton Skinner of Lanham, Md. and a daughter, Mrs. Anne Malone of Damascus, Md. and six grandchildren.

Funeral services were held Sept. 15 from Little River Baptist Church conducted by the Rev. Jesse Parker, pastor of the church. Burial was in Mt. Zion church cemetery.

The pallbearers were Herman Wright, John Fox, Enos Taylor, Edwin Skinner, Robert Byrne and James Kirkpatrick.

LOUDOUN TIMES-MIRROR
Leesburg, Virginia
Thursday, May 9, 1974

LOUIS CARTER

Louis Watson Carter, 56, of Aldie, died May 4 at Winchester Memorial Hospital. Mr. Carter was the owner of the Aldie Garage. A native of Loudoun County, he was the son of Annie Carter of Aldie and the late Ira Carter. Mr. Carter was a former fire chief of the Aldie Volunteer Fire Department.

Surviving besides his mother are his wife, Winifred Lee Carter; one son, Louis W. (Buzzy) Carter, of Aldie; one daughter, Mrs. Barbara Ann Williams of Leesburg; three sisters, Mrs. Ann McCarty of Silver Spring, Md., Mrs. Helen Meredith of Leesburg, and Miss Martha Carter of Aldie; and five grandchildren.

Funeral services were conducted May 7 from the Royston Funeral Home, Inc., Middleburg, with the Revs. Stuart Johnson and Neale Morgan officiating. Interment was in Mt. Zion Cemetery, Aldie.

LOUDOUN TIMES-MIRROR
Leesburg, Virginia
Thursday, January 15, 1976

SADIE HALL

Sadie Lee Hall, 73, of Middleburg, died Jan. 7 in Winchester Memorial Hospital after an extended illness. She was the wife of Franklin M. Hall.

Besides her husband, she is survived by two daughters, Mrs. Memphis Wolfe of Alexandria, Va. and Mrs. Margaret Tiffany of Middleburg and a son, Franklin Hall, Jr. of Hamilton. Other family members are brothers, five sisters, six grandchildren and four great-grandchildren. Funeral services were held at Royston's Funeral Home, Inc. in Middleburg on Jan. 10. Interment was in Mt. Zion Cemetery, Aldie.

LOUDOUN TIMES-MIRROR
Leesburg, Virginia
Thursday, April 1, 1976

EDWIN MARSHALL

Edwin Vincent Marshall, 82, died March 26 at his home in Aldie following a heart attack. Mr. Marshall was a retired painting contractor.

Surviving are his wife, Carrie Marshall; two step-daughters, Winifred Carter of Aldie and Mrs. Guy M. Fearnow of Maugansville, Md.; four step-grandchildren, Mrs. Alfred Williams, Jr., James Stenberg, Harry Bottorf III, and Buzzy Carter; and 11 great grandchildren.

Services were held March 29 at the Royston Funeral Home, Inc., Middleburg, with interment in Mt. Zion Cemetery, Aldie. The family asks that memorials be in the form of contributions to the Aldie Volunteer Fire Department, Aldie, Va.

LOUDOUN TIMES-MIRROR
Leesburg, Virginia
Thursday, April 15, 1976

ANNIE CARTER

Annie M. Carter, 83, wife of the late Ira C. Carter, died April 5 at her home in Aldie. Mrs. Carter was a daughter of Jacob and Rose Watson. Surviving are three daughters, Helen Meredith of Leesburg, Anne McCarty of Silver Spring, Md. and Miss Martha Carter of Aldie. 15 grandchildren and 21 great grandchildren. Services were held April 8 at the Aldie United Methodist Church with interment in Mt. Zion Cemetery, Aldie. Memorials may be in the form of contributions to the Aldie United Methodist Church Building Fund.

LOUDOUN TIMES-MIRROR
Leesburg, Virginia
Thursday, July 29, 1976

JOHN SKINNER

John Ludwell Skinner, 88, who spent the greater part of his life in the Little River section of Loudoun, died July 23 in Loudoun Memorial Hospital. He was a retired farmer and landowner. In earlier years he was active in Little River Baptist Church and the Ruritan Club. Mr. Skinner was the husband of the late Pamelia Lynn Ish Skinner, and the father of James M. Skinner of Lanham, Md. and Mrs. Ann Malone of Damascus, Md. He is also survived by six grandchildren. Services were held July 25 at the Little River Baptist Church and interment was in Mt. Zion Cemetery in Aldie. The family requests that memorial contributions be made to the Little River Baptist Church building fund. Arrangements were by Royston Funeral Home in Middleburg.

LOUDOUN TIMES-MIRROR
Leesburg, Virginia
Thursday, February 9, 1978

EULA BARTON

Eula Mae Barton, 82, of Chantilly, died Feb. 4 at Leesburg. She was the widow of Charles B. Barton. Mrs. Barton is survived by two sisters-in-law, Mrs. S. O. Burton and Mrs. Eva Flynn, both of Aldie, and a number of nieces and nephews. Funeral services were held Feb. 7 at the Royston Funeral Home, Middleburg. Interment was in Mt. Zion Cemetery, Aldie.

LOUDOUN TIMES-MIRROR
Leesburg, Virginia
Thursday, October 19, 1978

ALDIE FESTIVAL IS SET THIS WEEKEND

The harvest festival held annually in Aldie, will take place Saturday, Oct. 21, from 9 a.m. til 5 p.m. for the combined benefit of its churches and community organizations.

Located directly on Rte. 50 one mile west of Gilbert's Corner, at the foot of the Bull Run Mountains, Aldie is known for its historical association with statesmen like President James Monroe, and free-education advocate, Charles Fenton Mercer; the civil War Battle of Aldie, Col. John Mosby, and the Little River Turnpike itself.

A country dinner at the Aldie Fire House, including barbecued chicken, an old fashioned bazaar and luncheon at the Methodist Church, a sale of fresh and dried flowers and plants by the Aldie Horticultural Society, and a tour of the Aldie Mill are a part of the day's offerings, as are crafts demonstrations, pony rides and animal fair.

Harvest produce, pumpkins, apples, and vegetables -- summer's harvest of fruits, relishes, pickles -- cider straight from the mill -- cheeses, and freshly baked garnerings from local pantries . . . all in store for visitors.

LOUDOUN TIMES-MIRROR
Leesburg, Virginia
Thursday, October 26, 1978

RT. 50 WORK APPROVED

A project to continue the dual-laning of U.S. Rt. 50 in Loudoun County was approved last Thursday by the Highway and Transportation Commission.

Involved in the project will be the segment of Rt. 50 from a point near the intersection with Rt. 616, just southeast of Lenah, northwesterly to a point just southeast of Rt. 15, a distance of 2.6 miles.

Three possible locations for the project were studied to determine which would have the least effect on the community of Lenah. Various alignments, rights-of-way, and effect on the environment were considered for each of the three.

Scheme 1, one of the three presented for discussion at a public hearing last November, was approved by the commission. It provides for rebuilding the existing road at two locations where the alignment is poor. The first is just west of Lenah and is approximately 650 feet long. The second extends easterly from the end of the project for about 3,200 feet. The four-lane, divided facility will be provided by constructing two new traffic lanes on the north side of the existing road. The two roadways will be separated by a 65-foot median.

Some 7,745 vehicles use this segment of Rt. 50 a day. The 1995 anticipated traffic volume is 16,300 vehicles daily. The project is estimated to cost some $2,365,118. The Department of Highways and Transportation hopes to begin construction in 1979.

LOUDOUN TIMES-MIRROR
Leesburg, Virginia
Thursday, December 7, 1978

EFFA HUTCHISON, 91

Effa Grehan Hutchison, 91, a former Loudoun resident, died Dec. 2 at her Nashville, Tenn. home. Born in Franconia, she was a daughter of James Robert and Margaret Riticar Megeath.

Mrs. Hutchison was the wife of the late William Grehan and B. B. Hutchison. Surviving are two sons, Joe Grehan of Leesburg and James Grehan of Warrenton; two daughters, Hannah Byrd of Nashville and Margaret Crutchfield of Winston-Salem, N.C.; stepson, Louis S. Hutchison of Emporia and sister, June McCarty of New Baltimore; seven grandchildren and five great-grandchildren.

Services were held Dec. 4 from the Muse-Reed-Bange Funeral Home, Leesburg, with the Rev. Edgar Burkholder officiating. Interment was in Mt. Zion Church Cemetery, Aldie. Memorials may be made to the Aldie Volunteer Fire Department or the Arcola-Pleasant Valley Rescue Squad.

LOUDOUN TIMES-MIRROR
Leesburg, Virginia
Thursday, December 28, 1978

LELIA CONNOR

A funeral service for Mrs. **Lelia Carruthers Connor**, 94, a native of Loudoun, will be held from Ives Funeral Home at 2847 Wilson Blvd., Arlington, at 1 p.m. today (Thursday). Interment will be in Mt. Zion Cemetery, near Aldie, Va.

Mrs. Connor died in Arlington Hospital on Dec. 25. A daughter of Joel and Sarah T. Carruthers, whose home was Bull Run Farm, she was born Jan. 15, 1884. She was a member of the 8th Virginia Regiment and Arlington Chapters of the United Daughters of the Confederacy, Virginia Division, and for many years was a Chapter president. Her home was in Arlington.

Mrs. Connor was the aunt of Mrs. Margaret Dunn and Mrs. Frances G. Anderson of Winchester; Thomas Moore Carruthers of Charlottesville, Va. and Edward J. Carruthers of Chevy Chase, Md. She is survived by many great nieces and nephews. Her husband, James Robert Connor died in 1965.

LOUDOUN TIMES-MIRROR
Leesburg, Virginia
Thursday, April 2, 1981

RACHEL SHOCKLEY OF ARCOLA

Rachel Blanche Shockley, 75, of Arcola died March 30 at Loudoun Memorial Hospital. A native of The Plains, Mrs. Shockley was a retired postmistress at Arcola.

She was a member of the Arcola United Methodist Church where she also served on the church board. Mrs. Shockley was a member of the Dulles Doves Senior Citizens group.

Her husband, Jay Canada Shockley, died Aug. 13, 1957. Surviving are two daughters, Marian S. Wimer and Mary Virginia Shockley of Arcola; two sisters, Nettie Benton, Alexandria and Lena Miloki of Hampton; and four grandchildren.

Friends may call at the Muse and Reed Funeral Home, Leesburg, from 7-9 p.m. on Wednesday, April 1. Services will be held at 11 a.m. on Thursday, April 2, from the Arcola United Methodist Church with interment in the Mt. Zion Baptist Church Cemetery. The Revs. Richard Sisson and John Light will officiate. Memorials may be made to the Arcola United Methodist Church or the Arcola Rescue Squad.

Pallbearers will be Miles Shockley, Percy Benton, Sterling and Curtis Shockley, Raymond Downs and Les Pangle. Honorary pallbears will be James Kirkpatrick, Brooke Grimes, Edward Cornelius, Enock Slack, Flemming Lee, Robert Biggers, Joseph Cornelius and Dudley Webb.

LOUDOUN TIMES-MIRROR
Leesburg, Virginia
Thursday, March 25, 1982

LUTHER RUSH BOLT, WAS HOME
BUILDER HERE IN 1950'S

Luther Rush Bolt, 64, of Hamilton, a home builder during the 1950's and '60's in Loudoun, died March 17 at the Newton D. Baker Veterans Administration Hospital in Martinsburg, W.Va. He was a native of Sylvatus, Va.

Surviving are his wife, Sanalyn W. Bolt of the home; four children, Sharon A. Sazonick, Monroe, N. C., Christopher R., Harpers Ferry, W.Va., Martha E., Winchester, and John S. of the home.

Memorial services were held March 21 from Catoctin Presbyterian Church, Waterford, with the Rev. James E. Ammons officiating. Memorials may be made to the church memorial fund or the Hamilton Volunteer Rescue Squad. Arrangements by the Loudoun Funeral Chapel, Leesburg.

LOUDOUN TIMES-MIRROR
Leesburg, Virginia
Thursday, December 16, 1982

BILLY MEREDITH WAS SALESMAN

William (Billy) Harold Meredith, 37, a dispatcher and salesman for the Cherrydale Cement and Block Co. in Herndon, died Dec. 13 in Fairfax. He was a Leesburg resident.

Born Sept. 17, 1945 in Leesburg, Mr. Meredith was a son of Helen Carter Meredith of Leesburg and the late Robert Meredith. Surviving, in addition to his mother, are his wife, Sandra C. Meredith; two daughters, Tanya R. Meredith and Kristiana M. Elliott of Leesburg and one son, Steven T. Elliott, also of Leesburg; six sisters and brothers, Sandy K. Hackney, Paeonian Springs, Brenda M. Fulton and Wanda L. Carlson of San Diego, Calif., Jeanne M. Meadows, Elkton, Va., Bonnie M. McCue, Salisbury, Md. and Bruce D. Meredith, Sterling Park.

Friends may call at the Loudoun Funeral Chapel, Leesburg, from 7-9 p.m. Dec. 15 and 2-4 and 7-9 Dec. 16. Services will be held at 2 p.m. Friday, Dec. 17 from the Loudoun Funeral Chapel. Interment will be in Mt. Zion Baptist Church Cemetery, Aldie.

LOUDOUN TIMES-MIRROR
Leesburg, Virginia
Thursday, May 12, 1983

FRANKLIN HALL SERVICES

Franklin M. Hall Sr., 73, of Alexandria, the father of Franklin Hall Jr. of Hamilton, died May 6 at Mt. Vernon Hospital. He was the husband of the late Sadie Hall. Surviving, in addition to his son, are one sister, Mattilie Golivas of Mt. Rainier, Md. and two grandchildren. Graveside services were held May 9 from the Mt. Zion Cemetery, Aldie.

LOUDOUN TIMES-MIRROR
Leesburg, Virginia
Thursday, November 24, 1983

JACK CARTER, 52, SERVICES

Jack Carter, 52, of Leesburg, died Nov. 20 at Loudoun Memorial Hospital. Surviving are a son, Bruce Carter, Nokesville; two daughters, Melanie Hackney, Bluemont and Patricia Lynn Carter, Middleburg; one sister, Marian Leith, Leesburg and three grandchildren. Services will be held Wednesday, Nov. 23 at 1 p.m. from the Royston Funeral Home, Inc., Middleburg, with interment in Mt. Zion Cemetery, Aldie. Memorials may be made to the Northern Virginia Hospice, Loudoun Chapter.

LOUDOUN TIMES-MIRROR
Leesburg, Virginia
Thursday, October 3, 1985

MEMPHIS LEE WOLFE, FORMER RESIDENT

Memphis Lee Wolfe, 60, formerly of Loudoun County, died Sept. 29 at the Alexandria Hospital. She was a daughter of the late William Edward and Sadie Huff Jordan. Surviving are her husband, Granville Wolfe; one son, Jock Hunter Wolfe, Alexandria; one sister, Margaret Tiffany, Middleburg; and three grandchildren. Graveside services were held Oct. 2 from the Mt. Zion Baptist Church at Aldie.

LOUDOUN TIMES-MIRROR
Leesburg, Virginia
Thursday, January 23, 1986

DAISY JOHNSON HUTCHISON

Daisy Johnson Hutchison, 86, a retired teacher and Aldie resident, died Jan. 16 at the Rose Hill Nursing Home in Berryville. She was the wife of the late Carroll Smith Hutchison. Mrs. Hutchison is survived by cousins. Services were held Jan. 18 from the Royston Funeral Home, Middleburg, with interment in Mt. Zion Cemetery at Aldie.

POSEY F. PHILLIPS, 95, OF LEESBURG

Posey F. Phillips, 95, a retired carpenter and Leesburg resident, died Jan. 20 at Loudoun Memorial Hospital. Surviving are his wife, Christine S. Phillips; nine children, Posey Jr. and Robert J., Leesburg, Catherine Smith, Woodstock, Dorothy Myers, Hamilton, Marie Peterson, Ohio, Helen Neal, Florida, Hazel Moyer, Pennsylvania, Shirley R. Phillips, Harpers Ferry, Frankie Hawes, Baltimore; one brother, Lonnie J. Phillips, Leesburg. Services were held Jan. 22 from Colonial Funeral Home of Leesburg, with the Rev. L. D. Clemens officiating. Interment was in Mt. Zion Cemetery, Lenah.

LOUDOUN TIMES-MIRROR
Leesburg, Virginia
Thursday, October 29, 1987

ZELMA ROLLER MARSHALL, 84, HOMEMAKER

Zelma Roller Marshall, 84, longtime resident of Arcola, died Oct. 20 at Loudoun Memorial Hospital. Born Dec. 20, 1902, in Dowling, Ohio, she was the daughter of the late Jay C. and Maude Hampton Roller, who with their family were residents of Loudoun County from 1911 until 1923. Mrs. Marshall attended Madison Normal School in Harrisonburg and taught four years in the Pleasant Valley Elementary School. She was a member of Arcola United Methodist Church.

She married E. Ferne Marshall in 1924, and they lived in the family home for 63 years. Surviving, in addition to her husband, are three sons: Jay R. Marshall of Unionville, Richard F. Marshall of Arlington, Texas, Philip M. Marshall of Aldie; two daughters, Maude M. Henderson of Annandale and Carolyn M. Payne of Richmond; nine grandchildren; four great-grandchildren; 10 brothers and sisters who all formerly lived in Loudoun County, J. Hampton Roller of Scotch Ridge, Ohio, Dr. J. Paul Roller of Hilton Head, S.C., Howard Roller of Greensburg, Ind., Irene R. Liedel of Perrysburg, Ohio, Bernice R. Lunderman of Dayton, Ohio, Mary R. Eberhard and Ellen Roller, both of Toledo, Ohio, Joan R. Enright of Bowling Green, Ohio, Maude R. Fahle of Fremont, Ohio, and Hannah R. Cullis of Bryan, Ohio; and numerous nephews and nieces.

Funeral services were held Oct. 23 at Arcola United Methodist Church with interment in Mt. Zion Baptist Church Cemetery, Aldie. Pallbearers were her grandsons: Chris Marshall, Scott Marshall, Keith Marshall and John Payne. Also serving as pallbearers were: Bobby Biggers, Brook Grimes, Kenny Lowe, Dan Middleton and Enoch Slack. Memorial contributions may be made to the Arcola United Methodist Church Memorial Fund. Arrangements were by Loudoun Funeral Chapel, Leesburg.

LOUDOUN TIMES-MIRROR
Leesburg, Virginia
Thursday, November 10, 1988

CARRIE VIRGINIA MARSHALL, HOMEMAKER

Funeral services for **Carrie Virginia Marshall**, 85, were held Nov. 8 at Royston Funeral Home, Middleburg with the Rev. Carl Auel officiating. Interment was in Mt. Zion Cemetery, Aldie. Mrs. Marshall, a homemaker, was the wife of the late Edwin Vincent Marshall. She is survived by: two children, Winner Carter of Aldie and Ann Fearnow of Maugansville, Md.; one sister, Effie Seal of Martinsburg, W. Va.; four grandchildren, Buzzy Carter and Barbara Ann Williams, both of Aldie, Sandra Bottorf of LaPlata, Md. and Corinne Stenberg of Romney, W. Va.; 11 great-grandchildren; and two great, great-grandchildren. Memorial contributions may be made to the Aldie Volunteer Fire Department.

LOUDOUN TIMES-MIRROR
Leesburg, Virginia
Wednesday, April 25, 1990

SAVILLA PHILLIPS

Savilla Christine Phillips, 80, Round Hill, died April 22 at Loudoun Hospital Center.

Born March 30, 1910, in Virginia, she was the daughter of the late Henry C. and Lila Baker Jewell, the wife of the late Posey F. Phillips, the mother of the late Peggy Ann Phillips and the late Betty P. Lloyd, and the stepmother of the late Abraham C. Phillips. Mrs. Phillips was a homemaker.

Surviving are: five daughters, Hazel Moyer, Jonestown, Pa., Catherine Smith, Winchester, Dorothy P. Myers, Hamilton, Marie Peterson, Cincinnati, Ohio, and Helen Neil, Lutz, Fla.; three sons, Posey F. Phillips, Jr., Round Hill, Robert J. Phillips, Rippon, W. Va. and Shirley P. Phillips, Harpers Ferry, W. Va.; one stepdaughter, Frankie Hawes, Baltimore, Md.; one daughter-in-law, Paulette H. Phillips; 14 grandchildren; and seven great-grandchildren.

Funeral services will be held today at 2 p.m. at Colonial Funeral Home, Leesburg, with interment in Mount Zion Cemetery, Lenah.

LOUDOUN TIMES-MIRROR
Leesburg, Virginia
Thursday, August 13, 1992

JOHN JAY McCUE

John Jay McCue, 19, a Leesburg resident and a map coordinator with the U.S. Geological Survey, died Aug. 5 in Fairfax County.

Born Sept. 13, 1972, in Leesburg, he was the son of Bonnie M. McCue of Leesburg and Ronald Francis McCue of Salisbury.

Mr. McCue attended Loudoun County schools and was a 1990 graduate of Loudoun County High School where he was a member of the football team, wrestling squad and track team.

While in high school he worked for a time as manager of the Tally-Ho Theatre. He hoped to one day attend college and play college football.

Surviving, in addition to his parents, are two sisters, Stacey L. McCue of Sterling and Megan N. Meredith of Leesburg; one brother, Darryl L. McCue of Leesburg; and his maternal grandmother, Helen Carter Meredith of Leesburg.

Funeral services were conducted Aug. 9 at Loudoun Funeral Chapel, Leesburg with interment in Mount Zion Baptist Church Cemetery in Aldie.

Pallbearers were: Eric Johnson, Chris Williams, Tracy Marshall, Chris Hackney, Jason Hackney, Travis Hackney, Joey Kitts, Lance Green and Rob Grant.

LOUDOUN TIMES-MIRROR
Leesburg, Virginia
Thursday, January 9,1992

E. FERNE MARSHALL

E. Ferne Marshall, 93, Arcola, died Dec. 27 at his residence. Born Feb. 23, 1898, in Laurel Fork, he was the son of the late Isaac Monroe and Susannah Turman Marshall; and the husband of the late Zelma Roller Marshall who died Oct. 20, 1987.

Mr. Marshall attended the old Ashburn High School and served with the U.S. Navy during World War I. He farmed in the Arcola area throughout his lifetime. He was a former member of Arcola United Methodist Church where he served as a trustee. He served as a Loudoun County School Board member from 1948 to 1968 and on the Loudoun County A.S.C.S. Board for a number of years.

Mr. Marshall was a past director of Tri-County Electric Cooperative, and in that capacity he was instrumental in obtaining rural electric service for southeastern Loudoun County. He was recently recognized as a 71-year member of Ashburn Masonic Lodge AF&AM, Ashburn.

Surviving are three sons, Jay R. Marshall, Unionville, Richard F. Marshall, Arlington, Texas, and Philip M. Marshall, Aldie; two daughters, Maude M. Henderson, Annandale, and Carolyn M. Payne, Richmond; one sister, Glennie M. Fleming, Purcellville; nine grandchildren, Jay Christopher Marshall, Keith Frederick Marshall, Deborah M. Werner, Samuel M. Marshall, Elizabeth M. McBride, Lisa M. Decker, Leeanne M. Mountcastle, Elizabeth M. Payne and John T. Payne; and seven great-grandchildren.

Funeral services were conducted Dec. 30 at Loudoun Funeral Chapel in Leesburg with the Rev. William Martin officiating. Interment was in Mount Zion Cemetery, Aldie.

THE WASHINGTON POST
Washington, D.C.
Friday, January 12, 1996

SAMUEL EDWARD NEELY DIES;
ENGINEER WITH ARMY CORPS

Samuel Edward Neely, 90, who retired in 1963 as area engineer in charge of military construction for the military district of Washington after 28 years with Army Corps of Engineers, died Jan. 10 at the home of his daughter in Leesburg. He had Parkinson's disease.

Mr. Neely, a former resident of Silver Spring, had lived in the Washington area since 1952. He had homes in Leesburg and Jensen Beach, Fla.

Mr. Neely was born in McKees Rocks, Pa. He attended Carnegie Mellon University and was a graduate of the University of Pittsburgh.

He was an engineer with Fort Pitt Bridge Works in Pittsburgh early in his career. After he retired, he was an administrator in the construction division of the D.C. Department of Buildings and Grounds until 1966.

He was an elder of Northminster Presbyterian Church in Washington, a Mason, an instructor with the Potomac River Power Squadron and a member of the Anteaters Club.

Survivors include his wife of 61 years, Helen B. Neely of Leesburg and Jensen Beach; two children, Richard B. Neely of Ogden, Utah, and Joan N. Rippingale of Leesburg; five grandchildren; and a great-grandson.

CIVIL WAR SOLDIERS

Union

The Mount Zion Church Preservation Association erected twelve grave markers in 1997 for Union soldiers killed during the action at Mt. Zion Church on July 6, 1864. The Washington Evening Star for Saturday, July 9, 1864 reported:

"On receipt of the news, Colonel Lowell started off at midnight with 200 men from 2d and 13th regiments, and Captain McPherson, of 16th New York cavalry, joined him at Fairfax, and they proceeded to Aldie, where they found twenty-five wounded men, and eleven dead which they buried."

In a letter dated February 1865, Mrs. Alexander Davis wrote:

"Ellen (her daughter) saw eleven all buried in one grave last summer with coffins. They were buried a little over a mile from here where they fell. They belonged to Col. Lowell's Comm., fellow soldiers in the same reg. with your son & my husband. That was a skirmish with Mosby's Guerrillas."

The twelfth soldier recognized was Owen Fox, who was buried at a nearby farm house by the chaplain of the 2nd Massachusetts Cavalry who wrote:

"I borrowed a spade of the farmer and, selecting an attractive spot under a tree a little distance from the house, I began to dig a grave for the decent burial of the body of Owen Fox"

The names and units of those marked are as follows:

William F. Dumaresq	Co. K, 2nd Mass Cavalry
Owen Fox	Co. H, 2nd Mass Cavalry
Samuel C. Handscom	Co. A, 2nd Mass Cavalry
Michael Hubin	Co. I, 13tn NY Cavalry
John Johnson	Co. I, 2nd Mass Cavalry
Joseph Lovely	Co. K, 13th NY Cavalry
James McDonald	Co. F, 2nd Mass Cavalry
Duff Montando	Co. H, 13th NY Cavalry
Charles Oeldrailher	Co. G, 2nd Mass Cavalry
Patrick Riordan	Co. I, 2nd Mass Cavalry
Charles W. Rollins	Co. I, 2nd Mass Cavalry
Cornelius Tobin	Co. I, 2nd Mass Cavalry

Confederate

Several of those buried in the cemetery served with the Confederate army during the Civil War. Only the gravestone of William Hibbs indicates his service during the war. The names of these former soldiers and the units with which they served are listed below:

Charles W. Barton	1st VA Cavalry
William Hibbs	43rd VA Cavalry
A. Hamilton Lee	6th VA Cavalry
Thomas Litchfield	8th VA Infantry
John T. Lynn	43rd VA Cavalry
Jesse McIntosh	43rd VA Cavalry
Lewis F. Palmer	6th VA Cavalry
Robert A. Riticor	35th VA Cavalry
W. T. Saffer	6th VA Cavalry
James Sinclair	43rd VA Cavalry
Charles E. Skinner	8th VA Infantry
W. P. Thomas	43rd VA Cavalry
Philip F. Van Sickler	8th VA Infantry

One marker which was previously located at the cemetery was for J. T. Kelly who died September 4, 1862 of wounds at the 2nd Battle of Manassas. The marker is presently located in a private cemetery on Ticonderoga Farm. The base for the headstone and the footstone are still at Mt. Zion. When and why the headstone was removed is unknown.

MOUNT ZION CEMETERY

NAME	BORN	DIED	SECTION
ALLISON			
--Evelyn G.(*)	12 JUN 1886	27 JUN 1952	08-F
--Robert L.(*)	9 JUL 1885	5 APR 1960	08-E
ANDERSON			
--Georgia E.(*)	1863	1943	15-B
--Ira Imri	1852	1934	15-A
BADGER			
--Helen M.	1836	27 MAR 1882	33-03
--Joseph N.	21 MAR 1838	23 DEC 1914	33-04
--Maggie H.(*)	17 APR 1855	7 MAY 1943	33-05
BARTON			
--Charles B.(*)	13 SEP 1894	3 NOV 1969	24-C
--Charles W.(*)	1838	1926	24-A
--Ella Furr(*)	1870	1940	24-B
--Eula M.(*)	23 MAY 1895	4 FEB 1978	24-D
BOLT			
--C. B.	1895	1944	29-E
--Lillie Hurst(*)	16 OCT 1873	2 NOV 1954	29-C
--Luther Rush(*)	18 OCT 1917	17 MAR 1982	29-A
--Thomas J.	28 FEB 1863	17 DEC 1928	29-B
BRADSHAW			
--Rebecca W.	1 FEB 1829	12 DEC 1909	38-07
BRONAUGH			
--Sally(*)	21 JUL 1784	7 OCT 1869	31-07
BURTON			
--Elizabeth A.	23 OCT 1910	29 DEC 1941	08-G
CARRUTHERS			
--Joel		8 NOV 1911	20-A
--John G.(*)		7 DEC 1887	35-15
--Milton E.	1882	10 JAN 1912	35-16
--Sarah (THOMAS)(*)	24 NOV 1848	30 JUN 1930	20-B
CARTER			
--Annie (WATSON)(*)	28 JUL 1892	5 APR 1976	19-G
--Jack Bruce(*)	14 AUG 1931	20 NOV 1983	21-D
--Louis Watson(*)	25 AUG 1917	4 MAY 1974	19-H
--Sophia C.	6 DEC 1837	28 MAR 1900	34-05
COCKRILL			
--Annie J.	16 JUL 1854	11 MAY 1855	46-01

NAME	BORN	DIED	SECTION
COE			
--Elizabeth	30 MAY 1794	20 OCT 1869	30-02
--Infant	27 APR 1871	13 MAY 1871	30-01
--Robert	20 DEC 1789	16 SEP 1856	30-03
COLE			
--Rebecca C.	25 MAY 1813	3 AUG 1890	45-01
CONNOR			
--J. Robert(*)	1890	1965	19-A
--Lelia C.(*)	1884	1978	19-B
DANIEL			
--John Orr(*)	20 OCT 1863	25 NOV 1940	16-D
--Magnolia (SAFFER)(*)	16 MAR 1869	28 MAR 1940	16-E
DECKER			
--Jason Clark	12 FEB 1986	27 NOV 1987	23-I
DEMORY			
--Mary Margaret(*)	17 NOV 1840	6 APR 1906	36-07
DENEAL			
--Lucinda	1830	23 DEC 1885	50-1
DICKENS			
--Larry	1941	1942	29-D
EATON			
--David H. C.(*)	10 JAN 1844	8 MAR 1927	29-F
FERGUSON			
--Amanda V.	12 MAY 1837	11 JUN 1861	35-19
--Corinne Elizabeth	17 JUN 1885	25 DEC 1918	20-F
--Jack			20-G
--Josias	25 DEC 1812	8 NOV 1896	36-01
--Loraine(*)	20 JUN 1912	30 APR 1915	20-E
--Mary C.(*)	22 JAN 1846	31 OCT 1928	36-08
--Mary E.(*)	18 JUL 1883	25 JUL 1903	36-12
--Mary F.	15 APR 1818	20 MAY 1872	35-20
--Raymond K.	24 DEC 1888	7 NOV 1939	35-17
--W. L.	9 OCT 1850	13 APR 1913	35-18
--Welton	12 SEP 1878	29 JUL 1908	36-11
FLETCHER			
--Margaret Ella (RITICOR)	7 AUG 1848	1 JUN 1913	32-12
FOLEY			
--Mary E.	24 JAN 1828	5 SEP 1900	30-11
--Susan V.	2 APR 1836	11 NOV 1907	38-06
FRANCIS			
--Laura Page	15 DEC 1850	15 SEP 1897	35-04
--Willard Hume	10 SEP 1883	24 JAN 1892	35-05

NAME	BORN	DIED	SECTION
GALLEHER			
--George G.	1850	4 JAN 1908	33-09
--Harriet A.	16 JAN 1847	22 MAR 1904	33-08
--Sidney S.		16 APR 1883	33-07
GRAHAM			
--Mary E.	29 OCT 1859	12 APR 1944	31-01
GREEN			
--James C.(*)	1813	27 JAN 1876	32-06
--Lou(*)	16 JAN 1876	12 FEB 1931	50-2
--Toye W.	1807	1 FEB 1883	33-06
--Virginia F. T.(*)	17 MAY 1823	8 SEP 1905	32-07
GREHAN			
--Effa M.(*)	10 JUL 1887	2 DEC 1978	09-B
--William(*)	30 NOV 1883	13 FEB 1928	09-A
GULICK			
--Edna Jane	21 MAR 1850	7 MAY 1858	32-01
--Francis	3 APR 1822	18 OCT 1897	32-04
--Nancy	16 OCT 1821	1 DEC 1909	32-05
--Rosa Blanche	17 JUL 1860	17 APR 1861	32-02
HALL			
--Franklin M.(*)	1909	1983	22-F
--Sadie L.(*)	20 DEC 1902	7 JAN 1976	22-G
HENDERSON			
--Sherman D.	5 JUL 1911	21 AUG 1996	24-G
HIBBS			
--Major William(*)	1817	1887	40-03
--Martha		19 APR 1919	22-D
--Mary Jane (GOLDEN)(*)	1820	1882	40-04
HIXSON			
--Claudius T.(*)	27 DEC 1879	25 APR 1949	01-A
--Elizabeth (THOMAS)(*)	1 AUG 1862	24 JAN 1956	01-B
HOWERY			
--Mellie A.	28 JUL 1880	24 FEB 1964	01-C
HOWISON			
--Loudonia (MCINTOSH)	1839	1878	32-10
HUTCHISON			
--Blanche Beatty(*)	17 SEP 1903	4 MAR 1973	17-D
--Carroll Smith(*)	21 JUL 1897	8 JAN 1965	17-E
--Daisy (JOHNSON)(*)	12 MAY 1899	16 JAN 1986	17-F
--E. Dorman(*)	2 NOV 1863	17 JAN 1952	17-C
--Elizabeth(*)	1789	8 NOV 1875	30-05
--H. Ernest(*)	25 FEB 1899	11 JUL 1916	17-A
--Laura L. (SMITH)(*)	11 AUG 1864	23 JUN 1940	17-B
--Sampson	5 DEC 1775	9 OCT 1855	30-04

NAME	BORN	DIED	SECTION
ISBELL			
--Donald Duvall	27 AUG 1882	25 JUL 1954	15-E
--May Leon	8 APR 1887	7 MAY 1959	15-F
JAMES			
--Eleanora	21 DEC 1853	11 DEC 1922	38-03
--Harriet C.	29 MAR 1829	28 OCT 1902	38-04
--Sallie (CRAIN)	5 MAY 1786	14 DEC 1865	30-07
JENKINS			
--Helen A.	23 MAR 1898	15 NOV 1992	35-14
--Infant		26 JUL 1887	35-11
--J. Clay(*)	1859	6 FEB 1899	35-10
--Rosa Myrtle	24 SEP 1889	24 JAN 1890	35-12
--Roy Badger(*)	22 OCT 1891	10 FEB 1971	35-13
JOHNSON			
--Carrie V.(*)	10 JAN 1892	14 AUG 1970	08-B
--Elizabeth G.(*)	1857	1950	08-H
--Emma M.	5 JUL 1923	26 JUL 1923	08-D
--Jane C.	1802	2 MAR 1857	30-06
--Mary Eliza	1832	24 APR 1833	31-06
--Troylous F.(*)	29 AUG 1892	19 AUG 1956	08-C
--William A.(*)	1858	1928	08-I
JORDAN			
--Louise R.	16 SEP 1920	15 AUG 1921	22-I
--William E.(*)	6 MAY 1890	16 OCT 1939	22-H
KELLY			
--J. T.	21 JAN 1838	4 SEP 1862	37-01
--John(*)	29 MAR 1803	3 OCT 1866	37-02
KENDRICK			
--Louisa Ellen	1824	13 AUG 1882	34-16
LATHAM			
--Lucy M.		3 JUN 1858	33-01
LEE			
--A. Hamilton	29 MAY 1839	9 JUN 1904	31-11
--Ann	23 MAY 1808	1 MAR 1887	31-09
--John Berkeley(*)	14 APR 1834	17 NOV 1871	31-08
--Martha J.	14 APR 1834	23 JAN 1908	31-12
--Matthew P.(*)	4 SEP 1804	24 JAN 1896	31-10
LIGHTFOOT			
--Elizabeth	29 JAN 1826	9 AUG 1872	38-02
LITCHFIELD			
--Mary	27 MAY 1820	19 APR 1901	42-05
--Thomas W.	10 JUN 1842	8 FEB 1908	42-06

NAME	BORN	DIED	SECTION
LYNN			
--John T.(*)	1824	3 AUG 1872	43-05
--Nancy D.	12 OCT 1822	13 NOV 1907	43-04
--Thomas H. A.	21 APR 1850	11 JUN 1852	43-06
MARSDON			
--Mattie V.	1 JAN 1868	12 APR 1943	31-04
MARSHALL			
--Carrie V.(*)	19 AUG 1903	5 NOV 1988	09-D
--Edwin V.(*)	11 JUL 1894	26 MAR 1976	09-C
--Emmett Ferne(*)	23 FEB 1898	27 DEC 1991	23-G
--Isaac M.(*)	19 DEC 1873	23 MAR 1953	23-F
--Susannah T.(*)	12 MAR 1876	11 AUG 1931	23-E
--Zelma (ROLLER)(*)	20 DEC 1902	20 OCT 1987	23-H
MATTHEWS			
--Martha A.(*)	10 MAR 1840	4 NOV 1920	37-10
--Martin V.	1818	3 JUN 1895	37-09
MCCUE			
--John Jay(*)	13 SEP 1972	5 AUG 1992	21-G
MCFARLAND			
--Anastatia	23 AUG 1843	20 OCT 1882	41-01
--Florence T.(*)	1874	1 JUL 1896	42-03
--Sarah Jane	30 NOV 1845	3 JUL 1900	39-03
MCINTOSH			
--Ann Wood (HOWISON)		7 MAR 1864	32-09
--Catherine	1842	1853	32-11
--Jesse		15 JAN 1866	32-08
MEGEATH			
--Alfred	2 OCT 1809	11 JUL 1876	33-11
--James R.(*)	23 APR 1856	2 NOV 1926	16-F
--Margaret (RITICOR)(*)	10 APR 1857	15 AUG 1917	16-G
--Mary P. (HUMPHREY)(*)	7 JUL 1828	15 OCT 1920	33-10
MEREDITH			
--William H.(*)	17 SEP 1945	13 DEC 1982	21-H
MIDDLETON			
--Arthur W.	1852	1933	35-08
--Frances P.	2 OCT 1848	13 SEP 1883	35-02
--Howard		1936	34-04
--Infant			34-01
--Lovell H.	1805	13 DEC 1872	35-01
--Mary		1915	34-03
--Maude Thedolla	21 SEP 1889	4 NOV 1891	35-06
--Maury A.	29 MAY 1894	6 JAN 1904	35-07
--William			34-02

NAME	BORN	DIED	SECTION
MUNDAY			
--Thomas E.(*)	1852	7 DEC 1905	39-08
NEELY			
--Samuel Edward(*)	27 MAR 1905	10 JAN 1996	07-A
PALMER			
--Corbin F.	22 JAN 1876	22 JUN 1878	37-08
--Edna Annie	30 NOV 1876	5 JUN 1882	37-07
--L. F.(*)	3 OCT 1829	13 FEB 1892	37-06
--Mary E.	16 JUL 1843	12 FEB 1909	37-05
--Wallace H. F.	3 DEC 1883	19 MAR 1894	37-04
PETTITT			
--Susan C.	8 JAN 1860	24 DEC 1906	36-02
PHILLIPS			
--Abraham(*)	2 JUL 1912	18 OCT 1943	06-G
--Bertie H.	18 DEC 1888	14 FEB 1923	06-D
--Peggy Ann	3 MAR 1939	25 JAN 1940	06-H
--Posey F.(*)	29 0CT 1890	20 JAN 1986	06-F
--Savilla C.(*)	30 MAR 1910	22 APR 1990	06-E
PIERSON			
--Mary E. (HIBBS)	18 JAN 1846	10 OCT 1895	40-01
POWELL			
--Sallie (GULICK)		28 DEC 1928	09-H
PRESGRAVES			
--Eugene W.(*)	26 FEB 1855	15 DEC 1925	15-G
--Ida C.(*)	13 SEP 1857	8 SEP 1948	15-H
RITICOR			
--Charles(*)	7 JUL 1798	29 JUN 1877	33-13
--Charles A.(*)	20 SEP 1840	14 FEB 1873	32-14
--Elizabeth Jane (LEE)	29 SEP 1809	2 SEP 1877	32-15
--John(*)	30 MAY 1803	18 MAR 1888	32-16
--Joseph	17 MAR 1851	5 MAY 1914	32-18
--Malinda(*)	9 OCT 1809	28 JUN 1882	34-13
--Mary Catharine	5 JUL 1842	17 DEC 1907	32-13
--Robert A.	18 MAY 1844	12 MAR 1905	32-17
--Susan (MOSS)(*)	3 JAN 1815	26 OCT 1885	33-14
--Zilpha	2 FEB 1807	10 MAY 1891	34-14
SAFFER			
--Rosa B.	19 MAR 1865	2 DEC 1886	34-07
--Ruth E. (TAVENNER)(*)	1840	15 JUL 1897	34-10
--Viola D.(*)	30 MAR 1884	25 FEB 1886	34-08
--W. T.(*)	1826	17 JAN 1894	34-09
SAULS			
--Sarah Catherine	24 NOV 1900	1900	42-04

NAME	BORN	DIED	SECTION
SHOCKLEY			
--Canada H.	18 DEC 1849	7 MAR 1932	03-F
--James M.(*)	1899	1970	03-C
--Jay C.(*)	1894	1957	03-G
--Lucie M.(*)	1900	1967	03-D
--Mary N.	7 NOV 1862	3 NOV 1917	03-E
--Rachel D.(*)	1905	1981	03-H
SILCOTT			
--James Henry	13 SEP 1820	7 MAY 1905	31-02
--Martha (EWERS)	23 JAN 1830	16 NOV 1901	31-03
--William H.(*)	1863	1920	31-05
SINCLAIR			
--Father(*)	1833	1926	39-05
--Mother	1848	1906	39-06
--Son	1872	1891	39-07
--Susan		17 DEC 1919	33-12
SKINNER			
--Charles E.(*)	7 DEC 1840	15 AUG 1922	05-F
--John L.(*)	13 JUN 1888	23 JUL 1976	05-B
--Laura M.(*)	7 SEP 1856	11 AUG 1933	05-E
--Pamelia I.(*)	24 FEB 1888	13 SEP 1973	05-C
--Ruth Earl(*)	25 MAR 1931	22 SEP 1933	05-A
STEADMAN			
--Lelia	9 MAY 1855		04-H
STEPHENSON			
--Catherine L.	1 FEB 1812	13 JUN 1900	39-02
--William H.	8 MAR 1816	11 MAR 1888	39-01
SUMMERS			
--Margaret	1841	8 SEP 1915	30-12
TAVENNER			
--Jonah	1815	30 APR 1893	34-06
TAYLOR			
--Sallie N. (COLE)	1843	11 APR 1883	45-02
THOMAS			
--Alice Pangle(*)	1898	1931	18-G
--Charles W.(*)	1881	1961	20-D
--Griffeth E.(*)	16 MAR 1814	11 OCT 1899	36-05
--Henry Phineas(*)	22 MAY 1894	23 MAY 1969	18-E
--John G.(*)	1884	1951	18-F
--Rebecca B.	10 OCT 1821	15 SEP 1911	36-06
--Rebecca May(*)	1886	1933	20-C

NAME	BORN	DIED	SECTION
THOMAS			
--Sallie (RITICOR)(*)	25 JUL 1851	28 NOV 1919	18-I
--Virginia Ann(*)	1926	1928	18-H
--William Phineas	6 NOV 1845	8 JUL 1915	18-J
THOMPSON			
--Edward(*)	28 JAN 1803	17 DEC 1886	39-04
TRAMMELL			
--Horace	1910	1981	22-E
TRIPLITTE			
--Margaret (RITICOR)(*)	28 FEB 1811	6 AUG 1882	34-12
TURMAN			
--John W.	25 MAY 1909	16 FEB 1911	43-01
UTTERBACK			
--Helen F.	11 JUL 1916	20 DEC 1918	04-G
VANSICKLER			
--Margaret(*)	13 OCT 1865	8 APR 1898	38-05
--Philip F.(*)	17 SEP 1838	19 NOV 1913	16-A
--Sarah P.(*)	21 OCT 1838	29 JUL 1927	16-B
--William H.	9 OCT 1879	27 JAN 1937	16-C
WALKER			
--Angelina	30 SEP 1820	29 DEC 1899	36-13
WALL			
--Guy Melton	27 SEP 1892	13 AUG 1893	35-03
WARD			
--Elizabeth Jane	1 FEB 1836	11 MAR 1907	37-11
WATSON			
--Jacob B.	6 MAR 1842	15 SEP 1919	19-E
--Rose Everett(*)		1938	19-F
WHALEY			
--Mary A.	5 JUN 1800	19 JUN 1881	30-10
WOLFE			
--Memphis(*)	14 APR 1925	29 SEP 1985	22-C
WOODY			
--Angie F.	1880	1973	36-10
--Jarvis J.	1883	1958	36-09
YOUNG			
--Emma H.	1865	1 JUL 1916	35-09

(*) death notice, obituary or news item included in text.

82

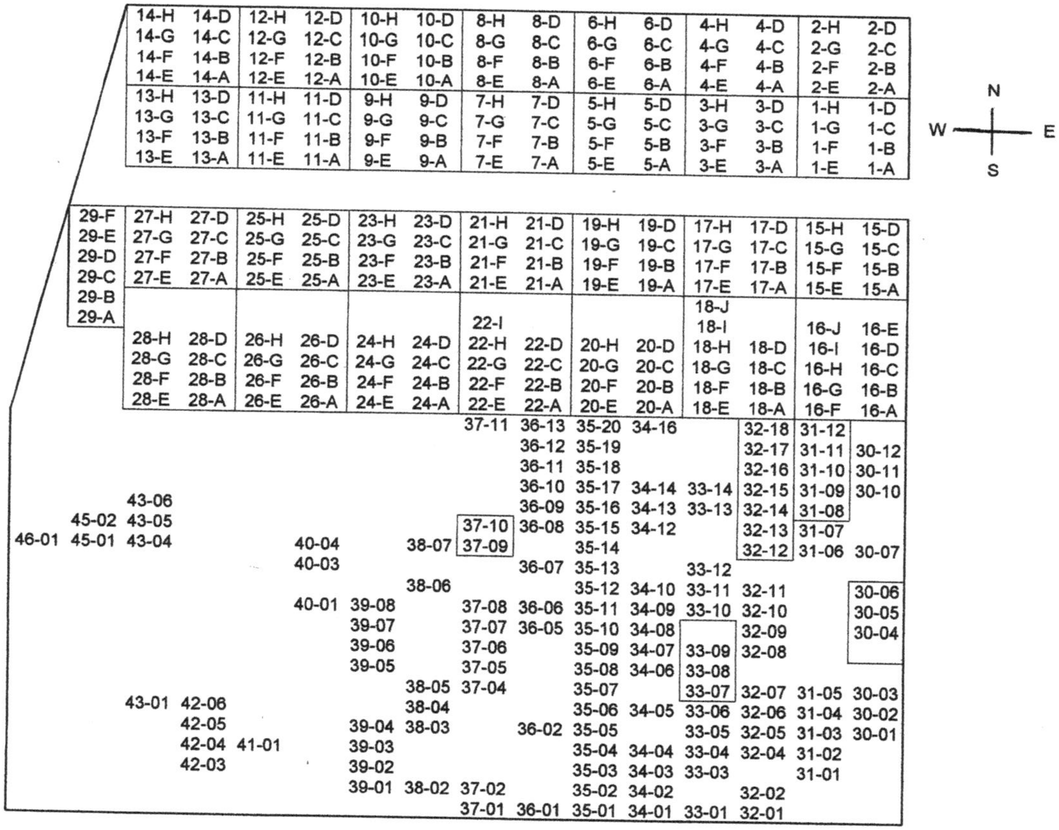

MOUNT ZION CEMETERY
circa 1852

Compass: N (left), E (up), W (lower-left), S (down)

Lettered sections (plots):

Section	Plots
1	1-A, 1-B, 1-C, 1-D, 1-E, 1-F, 1-G, 1-H
2	2-A, 2-B, 2-C, 2-D, 2-E, 2-F, 2-G, 2-H
3	3-A, 3-B, 3-C, 3-D, 3-E, 3-F, 3-G, 3-H
4	4-A, 4-B, 4-C, 4-D, 4-E, 4-F, 4-G, 4-H
5	5-A, 5-B, 5-C, 5-D, 5-E, 5-F, 5-G, 5-H
6	6-A, 6-B, 6-C, 6-D, 6-E, 6-F, 6-G, 6-H
7	7-A, 7-B, 7-C, 7-D, 7-E, 7-F, 7-G, 7-H
8	8-A, 8-B, 8-C, 8-D, 8-E, 8-F, 8-G, 8-H
9	9-A, 9-B, 9-C, 9-D, 9-E, 9-F, 9-G, 9-H
10	10-A, 10-B, 10-C, 10-D, 10-E, 10-F, 10-G, 10-H
11	11-A, 11-B, 11-C, 11-D, 11-E, 11-F, 11-G, 11-H
12	12-A, 12-B, 12-C, 12-D, 12-E, 12-F, 12-G, 12-H
13	13-A, 13-B, 13-C, 13-D, 13-E, 13-F, 13-G, 13-H
14	14-A, 14-B, 14-C, 14-D, 14-E, 14-F, 14-G, 14-H
15	15-A, 15-B, 15-C, 15-D, 15-E, 15-F, 15-G, 15-H
16	16-A, 16-B, 16-C, 16-D, 16-E, 16-F, 16-G, 16-H, 16-I, 16-J
17	17-A, 17-B, 17-C, 17-D, 17-E, 17-F, 17-G, 17-H
18	18-A, 18-B, 18-C, 18-D, 18-E, 18-F, 18-G, 18-H, 18-I, 18-J
19	19-A, 19-B, 19-C, 19-D, 19-E, 19-F, 19-G, 19-H
20	20-A, 20-B, 20-C, 20-D, 20-E, 20-F, 20-G, 20-H
21	21-A, 21-B, 21-C, 21-D, 21-E, 21-F, 21-G, 21-H
22	22-A, 22-B, 22-C, 22-D, 22-E, 22-F, 22-G, 22-H, 22-I
23	23-A, 23-B, 23-C, 23-D, 23-E, 23-F, 23-G, 23-H
24	24-A, 24-B, 24-C, 24-D, 24-E, 24-F, 24-G, 24-H
25	25-A, 25-B, 25-C, 25-D, 25-E, 25-F, 25-G, 25-H
26	26-A, 26-B, 26-C, 26-D, 26-E, 26-F, 26-G, 26-H
27	27-A, 27-B, 27-C, 27-D, 27-E, 27-F, 27-G, 27-H
28	28-A, 28-B, 28-C, 28-D, 28-E, 28-F, 28-G, 28-H
29	29-A, 29-B, 29-C, 29-D, 29-E, 29-F

Numbered sections (plots):

Section	Plots
30	30-01, 30-02, 30-03, 30-04, 30-05, 30-06, 30-07, 30-10, 30-11, 30-12
31	31-01, 31-02, 31-03, 31-04, 31-05, 31-06, 31-07, 31-08, 31-09, 31-10, 31-11, 31-12
32	32-01, 32-02, 32-04, 32-05, 32-06, 32-07, 32-08, 32-09, 32-10, 32-11, 32-12, 32-13, 32-14, 32-15, 32-16, 32-17, 32-18
33	33-01, 33-03, 33-04, 33-05, 33-06, 33-07, 33-08, 33-09, 33-10, 33-11, 33-12, 33-13, 33-14
34	34-01, 34-02, 34-03, 34-04, 34-05, 34-06, 34-07, 34-08, 34-09, 34-10, 34-12, 34-13, 34-14, 34-16
35	35-01, 35-02, 35-03, 35-04, 35-05, 35-06, 35-07, 35-08, 35-09, 35-10, 35-11, 35-12, 35-13, 35-14, 35-15, 35-16, 35-17, 35-18, 35-19, 35-20
36	36-02, 36-05, 36-06, 36-07, 36-08, 36-09, 36-10, 36-11, 36-12, 36-13
37	37-01, 37-02, 37-04, 37-05, 37-06, 37-07, 37-08, 37-09, 37-10, 37-11
38	38-01, 38-02, 38-03, 38-04, 38-05, 38-06, 38-07
39	39-01, 39-02, 39-03, 39-04, 39-05, 39-06, 39-07, 39-08
40	40-01, 40-03, 40-04
41	41-01
42	42-03, 42-04, 42-05, 42-06
43	43-01, 43-04, 43-05, 43-06
45	45-01, 45-02
46	46-01

RITICOR

Amasa Riticor m. 1795 Catherine Pullin

Charles
b. 1796
d. 1877

m. 1842
Susanna Moss
d. 1885

John
b. 1803
d. 1888

m. 1839
Elizabeth Jane Lee
d. 1877

Zilpha
b. 1807
d. 1891

Malinda
b. 1809
d. 1882

Margaret
b. 1811
d. 1882

m. 1854
Richard Triplett

Charles Riticor   m.   1842   Susanna Moss

Elizabeth A.
b. 1843

John Thomas
b. 1845

Elijah V.
b. 1847

Sallie A.
b. 1851
d. 1919

m. 1877
William Phineas Thomas
d. 1915

Charles F.
b. 1854

Margaret E.
b. 1857
d. 1917

m. 1886
James Robert Megeath
d. 1926

John Riticor m. 1839 Elizabeth Jane Lee

Charles Alexander
b. 1840
d. 1873

Mary Catherine
b. 1842
d. 1907

m. 1890
David H. C. Eaton
d. 1927

Robert A.
b. 1844
d. 1905

Joshua L.
b. 1846

Margaret Ella
b. 1848
d. 1913

Joseph
b. 1851
d. 1914

Bold indicates buried in Mt. Zion Cemetery

CHART NO. 1

SAFFER

Jonah Tavenner
d. 1893   m. 1838   Sarah Jane Baldwin

Ruth Emma
b. 1839
d. 1897

m. 1860
William Thornton Saffer
d. 1894

William Thornton Saffer   m. 1860   Ruth Emma Tavenner

Lillie
b. 1861

Rose B.
b. 1865
d. 1886

Gertrude
b. 1867

m. 1885
John Frank Gulick

Magnolia
b. 1869
d. 1940

m. 1887
John Orr Daniel
d. 1940

Osceola
b. 1871

Claude
b. 1873

m. 1898
Olive May Riticor

William Clinton
b. 1876

Viola D.
b. 1884
d. 1886

Bold indicates buried in Mt. Zion Cemetery

CHART NO. 2

THOMAS

Griffith E. Thomas d. 1899 — m. 1838 — **Rebecca B. Wright** d. 1911

- Mary M. b. 1842
- Ann C. b. 1844
- **William Phineas** b. 1845 d. 1915
  - m. 1877
  - **Sallie A. Riticor** d. 1919
- **Sarah** b. 1848 d. 1930
  - m.
  - **Joel Carruthers** d. 1914
- John C. b. 1851
- Edwin b. 1854
- Charles b. 1856
- Tarleton B. b. 1859
- **Elizabeth** b. 1862 d. 1956
  - m.
  - **Claudius T. Hixson** d. 1949

William P. Thomas — m. 1877 — Sallie A. Riticor

- Clarence R.
- **Charles W.** b. 1881 d. 1961
  - m.
  - **Rebecca May Carruthers** d. 1933
- **John G.** b. 1884 d. 1951
  - m.
  - **Alice Pangle** d. 1931
- Mabel E. b. 1887
- Susie b. 1889
- **Henry P.** b. 1894 d. 1969
- Margaret S. b. 1896

Joel Carruthers — m. — Sarah F. Thomas

- Elmer I. b. 1874
- Blanche b. 1878
- **Lelia E.** b. 1884 d. 1978
  - m.
  - **J. Robert Connor** d. 1965
- **Rebecca May** b. 1887 d. 1933
  - m.
  - **Charles W. Thomas** d. 1961
- Pearl E. b. 1889

Bold indicates buried in Mt. Zion Cemetery

CHART NO. 3

MEGEATH

Alfred Megeath
d. 1876

m. 1850

Mary P. Humphrey
d. 1920

Herbert
b. 1851

Blanche
b. 1854

James R.
b. 1856
d. 1926

Lelia Ann
b. 1857

Flora
b. 1860

Gabriel
b. 1866

Alfred P.
b. 1870

m. 1886
Margaret E. Riticor
d. 1917

m.
John Ferguson

m.
James Ferguson

m.
J. Marvin Leith

James R. Megeath   m. 1886   Margaret E. Riticor

Effa
b. 1887
d. 1978

Mary June
b. 1890

Jessie
b. 1893

Robert Humphrey
b. 1899

m. 1916
William Grehan
d. 1928

Bold indicates buried in Mt. Zion Cemetery

CHART NO. 4

FERGUSON

Josias Ferguson
d. 1896

m. 1837

Mary Frances Kerchevale
d. 1872

Amanda
b. 1839
d. 1861

Kate
b. 1842

Mary
b. 1844

Welton L.
b. 1850
d. 1913

m.
Mary C.
d. 1928

Welton L. Ferguson   m.   Mary C.

Welton L. Jr.
b. 1878
d. 1908

Angie
b. 1880
d. 1973

m.
Jarvis Woody
d. 1958

Mary Ethel
b. 1883
d. 1903

Herbert W.
b. 1885

m.
Corinne E.
d. 1918

Loraine
b. 1912
d. 1915

Raymond K.
b. 1888
d. 1939

Bold indicates buried in Mt. Zion Cemetery

CHART NO. 5

BARTON - JOHNSON

Charles W. Barton
d. 1926

m.

Ella Furr
d. 1940

Nellie
b. 1898

Eva
b. 1900

m.
Stuart O. Burton

m.
Carroll Flynn

Charles B.
b. 1894
d. 1969

William Amos Johnson
d. 1928

m.

Elizabeth Griffith
d. 1950

Emma
b. 1889

Mary E.
b. 1890

Troylous
b. 1892
d. 1956

Eula
b. 1895
d. 1978

William G.
b. 1900

Evelyn G
b. 1886
d. 1952

m.
Carrie V. Lee
d. 1970

m.
Charles Barton
d. 1969

m.
Robert Allison
d. 1960

Bold indicates buried in Mt. Zion Cemetery

CHART NO. 6

Laura Smith, 43, 51, 56, 60
Louis S., 65
Mary, 43
Mrs. B. B., 55
Mrs. Ludwell, 24
Mrs. T. B., 42
Mrs. Westwood, 40
Sampson, 4
T. Gales, 51
William, 16

I

Isbell, May L., 46
  Mrs. Don, 23
Ish, 50
  Edgar, 61
  Milton, 43, 51
  Pamelia Lynn, 61

J

Jackson, Guy, 48
  Skinny, 48
Jenkins, Clay, 36, 60
  Elmer, 60
  Emma, 60
  Helen A., 60
  James Clay, 13
  Roger, 54
  Roy B., 60
  W. S., 13
  William, 13
Jewell, Henry C., 70
  Lila Baker, 70
Johnson, Amos, 32, 54
  Carrie V., 59
  Carrie Virginia, 54
  Charles, 45
  Donnie, 59
  Elizabeth, 47
  Elizabeth Griffith, 33, 51, 54
  Eric, 70
  Eula, 33
  Grafton, 47, 51
  John, 73

John A., 54, 59
Rev. Stuart, 61
Robert, 59
T. F., 33
Troylous, 47, 51, 59
Troylous Franklin, 54
W. G., 33
William Jr., 59
William Amos, 33, 47, 51
William H., 54, 59
Jones, Lina, 10
Jordan, Sadie Huff, 68
  William Edward, 68
Jordon, Marguerite, 41
  Memphis, 41
  William, 41

K

Keith, Judge, 8
Kelly, J. T., 74
  John, 2
Kerr, Elder H. C., 31, 40
Ketland, Mary, 59
Kirk, Bud, 48
Kirkpatrick, James, 54, 61, 66
Kitts, Joey, 70
Knight, Dorothy, 17

L

Lacey, Hasel, 42
  Joe, 42
  Veda Lee, 52
Laws, Dr. T. L., 3
Leachman, Elder Robert C., 50
Lee, 50
  A. H., 11
  A. Hamilton, 74
  B. Frank, 59
  Berkley, 52
  Charles, 59
  David C., 59
  Flemming, 66

Mrs. John, 41
Thrift, Walter, 15
Tiffany, Margaret, 62, 68
Tobin, Cornelius, 73
Topping, Elder D. L., 31, 40
Trainham, Rev. C. Wirt, 23, 40
Trenary, 48
Triplett, Margaret, 6
Turman, Alice, 36
  C. M., 16, 36, 45
  Dr. A. E., 36
  Dr. J. W., 36
  Dr. O. F., 36
  James M., 36
  Tabitha, 36
Turner, Elder C. E., 50
  William, 17
Tyler, Carroll F., 30
  Estelle, 27
  Olivia, 27
  Squire, 19
  W. E., 27

V

Vansickler, E. H., 13
  E. Holmes, 29
  Frank, 16
  Joseph, 16
  Margaret, 13
  Philip F., 74
  Sarah Davis, 29
Vaughn, Elder C. W., 16, 31, 40
  Ona, 16

W

Waddell, 48
Walker, Elder T. W., 31, 40
  Miss Henrie, 19
Waters, Mrs. W. W., 42
  Susie, 44
  William, 44
Watson, Jacob, 62

Jacob B., 41
Rose, 62
Rose Powell, 41
William, 41
Weaver, Elder George, 50
Webb, Dudley, 66
Weimer, John W., 57
Welsh, Samuel, 47
Werner, Deborah M., 71
Whaley, C. A., 32
  C. W., 47
  S. J., 32
  William, 32
Williams, Barbara Ann, 61, 69
  Chris, 70
  Mrs. Alfred Jr., 62
  Virgil, 37
Wilson, Stanley E., 56
Wimer, Marian S., 66
Wolfe, Granville, 68
  Jock Hunter, 68
  Memphis, 62
  Memphis Lee, 68
Wood, Elder J. D., 49, 50, 52, 53, 55, 57, 59
Wortman, Carl, 15
  May, 15
  Mrs. L. J., 15
  Stanley, 57
Wright, Herman, 61
  Rev., 33
Wyckoff, A. C., 17

Y

Yoeman, Mr., 15
York, Rev. J. M., 38
Young, Lindsay, 27